Seneca: Phaedra

DUCKWORTH COMPANIONS
TO GREEK AND ROMAN TRAGEDY

Seneca: Phaedra

Roland Mayer

Duckworth

First published in 2002 by
Gerald Duckworth & Co. Ltd.
61 Frith Street, London W1D 3JL
Tel: 020 7434 4242
Fax: 020 7434 4420
Email: inquiries@duckworth-publishers.co.uk
www.ducknet.co.uk

© 2002 by Roland Mayer

All rights reserved. No part of this publication
may be reproduced, stored in a retrieval system, or
transmitted, in any form or by any means, electronic,
mechanical, photocopying, recording or otherwise,
without the prior permission of the publisher.

A catalogue record for this book is available
from the British Library

ISBN 0 7156 3165 9

Typeset by Ray Davies
Printed in Great Britain by
Biddles Ltd, *www.biddles.co.uk*

Contents

Preface	7
1. Seneca and Roman Tragedy	9
2. The Action of the Play	19
3. The Major Themes of the Play	37
4. Characterisation	51
5. Literary Texture	65
6. Reception and Later Influence	75
7. Interpretation	89
8. Performance History	97
9. Translations	105
Notes	111
Guide to Further Reading	125
Bibliography	131
Chronology	139
Index	141

For Michael Coffey

Preface

When the editor of this series invited me to contribute to it a study of Seneca's *Phaedra*, I readily welcomed the opportunity to discuss once again this dramatic text, but now with a different sort of reader in mind. A decade and more ago my friend and colleague, Michael Coffey, and I produced for the Cambridge Greek and Latin Classics series, an edition of the *Phaedra* with an introduction and a commentary on the Latin text. This of course restricted our readership and our aims. The scope of the present series is much wider, and I am happy to have the chance not only to make good some omissions in the earlier presentation of the play, but to address as well fresh aspects of the piece, for instance, its performance and wider reception, that were beyond the scope of that earlier undertaking. Moreover, scholarly work on Senecan drama continues (though not quite unabated, compared to the 1980s), and aspects of our play have been dealt with in a number of journal articles to which attention can usefully be drawn. There is still only one other book dedicated exclusively to *Phaedra*, that by the late Charles Segal, and so another short analysis of the play, with up to date bibliography, ought to fill a real need among students of Roman drama, and of drama generally.

King's College London   R.M.
2002

1
Seneca and Roman Tragedy

Seneca's life and writings

Lucius Annaeus Seneca was born shortly before the Christian era – the exact date is not known – in the Roman province of Baetica, in southern Spain, at Corduba (modern Córdoba). His father, who bore the same name, was a wealthy *eques* (literally 'knight'; a member of the non-political propertied élite), with a passionate interest in contemporary rhetorical practice. To ensure that his son received an up-to-date training as an orator he took him to Rome, where he was apprenticed to Papirius Fabianus (Seneca himself describes the man's oratory and philosophical interests in his Letter 100). Such an education was designed to fit a man for public life, and not surprisingly Seneca, who practised at the Roman bar, also began a political career by holding the magistracy known as 'quaestor'; the date when he held the office is not known, but it was under either the emperor Tiberius or his nephew Gaius (more familiarly known as Caligula). His career was checked in the first year of the reign of Claudius (41), whose wife Messalina seems to have instigated against Seneca a charge of adultery with the emperor's niece, Julia Livilla; he was condemned, but exiled to Corsica rather than executed. He had poor health and was possibly tubercular, and it may be that Claudius believed the disease would finish him off, sparing the need to execute him. This must have been a bleak time in Seneca's life, from which he cannot have been sure that he would ever be released (like the poet Ovid, whom Tiberius did not recall from the exile imposed upon him by Augustus; emperors tended to respect their predecessor's judgements wherever possible).

But in 49 Claudius had a new wife, Agrippina, and she had Seneca recalled to teach her son, Nero, the arts of oratory, in which he was an acknowledged master. Seneca was now appointed to the office of praetor, and when his pupil became emperor in 54, he rewarded Seneca with the highest magistracy, the consulship, in 55 or 56. Seneca's role at court was very much that of a guardian, as well as occasional speech-writer for Nero. Since he had to adopt the persona of the emperor, we may see in this exercise a talent that to some extent fits a dramatist as well, the ability to take on another's character.

When Agrippina was executed in 59, Seneca even had to write on Nero's behalf the letter to the Senate in which the act was justified. He continued to serve Nero until the death in 62 of the prefect of the Praetorian Guard (the emperor's personal troops), Afranius Burrus, who had from the first been equal partner with him in trying to direct and control Nero's character. In that year Seneca realised that retirement from public life would be the safest course, and he received Nero's permission to give himself up to leisure, perhaps on one of his estates away from Rome.

In 65 a notable conspiracy of aristocrats, centred on Lucius Calpurnius Piso, was uncovered, and Seneca, who may have been aware of it, was at any rate implicated. He knew that his end was near, and in 66 arranged his suicide with a philosophical resolution worthy of Socrates. The scene is one of the most memorable described by Tacitus (*Annals* 15.60.3-64.6).[1]

Seneca's official literary activities have already been hinted at, but he worked in many other genres, chiefly prose, and prose of a philosophical character at that. For Seneca was a committed Stoic, and used his writings, especially the engaging *Letters* to Lucilius, composed during his retirement, to advocate a

1. Seneca and Roman Tragedy

heightened engagement with ethical concerns in his readers. We do not possess all of his philosophical compositions; many have been lost. But his dedication to Stoic teaching is often felt to have had some influence upon his dramatic writing, so it should always be borne in mind. A few words about the main tenets of the philosophy will therefore be in order here.

Stoicism was a system, that is to say, it tried to give a comprehensive and integrated account of the world and of man's place in it. The foundation of the system was the proposition that the world is ordered in accordance with the rational will of god; whatever happens must accord with that will, and nature (*phusis* in Greek, *natura* in Latin) is thus in itself a primary good. Man's goal is to realise virtue (*arete* in Greek, *virtus* in Latin), and the high road to that goal is a life in accordance with nature. Reason (*logos* in Greek, *ratio* in Latin), which permeates the world, guides us to what is right. But it is opposed by passion, a defect brought about by mistaken judgment. But whatever man gets up to for good or ill, overall is the benevolent will of god, which takes the form of providence. There is, in the Stoic system, no such thing as blind chance (*fortuna* in Latin), since all is fated by divine foreknowledge, which acts for the universal good. The doctrines sketched here have a clear bearing on tragic sensibility, but the correspondence of Stoicism and tragedy is harder to chart, as we shall see in due course.[2]

As a writer of prose, Seneca held a remarkable position, still acknowledged (grudgingly) a generation later by the teacher of oratory, Quintilian.[3] Seneca developed a crisp, flexible, epigrammatic style that was the antithesis of the earlier elaborate style which was associated above all with the orator Cicero.[4] This compact style was well adapted to essays and letters, brief expositions of moral issues. The obvious defect in Seneca's prose works is a lack of overall shape; he tends to repetitiveness, especially evident in the three-book treatise on anger. This indifference to form is also detectable in his dramas, which tend to fall into unconnected scenes rather than to be built in a single arc.

This concern with parts rather than the whole in fact characterises the literature of his age. Seneca lived at a time, especially under Nero, when literature went through a second Golden Age, thanks especially to the emperor's enthusiasm for all matters artistic. Nero himself as we know took to composing poetry, and it is possible that Seneca may have introduced to the emperor's notice his nephew, the epic poet Lucan. Nero's passion was the drama, in which he liked to perform, in the original Greek, roles of a specially pathetic nature, for example, Niobe, Canace's birth pangs, the blinded Oedipus, and the raving Hercules (Suetonius, *Life of Nero* 21.3); the last two were roles recreated for the Roman stage by Seneca. Here too we note the contemporary fashion for 'bleeding chunks', hacked off the body of a play for concert performance, another inducement to focus upon the scene rather than the integrated plot of the whole drama.[5]

Like many educated Romans, for example Cicero and his brother Quintus, Seneca was adroit at composing in verse: we find verse passages reminiscent of some choral odes of his tragedies in the scathing satire upon the deification of the emperor Claudius, entitled *Apocolocyntosis*. Cicero himself had sometimes produced translations of speeches from Greek tragedies, and his brother (as will be noted again below) knocked off a few scripts as a literary exercise while serving in Gaul under Julius Caesar. Seneca however is no translator; the original Greek plays are springboards for his imagination, and are nowhere closely followed. As we shall see, he combines scenes from a variety of dramas with passages inspired by other poetic (often non-dramatic) sources.

We cannot say when Seneca began to compose tragedies in earnest. We find a reference in Quintilian (*Institutio oratoria*

1. Seneca and Roman Tragedy

8.3.31) to his discussion of the use in tragedy of a particular word, *elimino* 'I turn out of doors', which Quintilian heard as a young man; the occasion is usually dated to the late 40s or early 50s of the reign of Claudius. Thanks to the investigation of sense-pauses in the dramas by J.G. Fitch, a relative chronology of the extant (and authentic) plays is generally accepted.[6] *Phaedra* is deemed to be early, and is dated provisionally to the final years of Claudius: this is important because it rules out any interpretation of the text which depends upon the presence of specific allusions to Nero and Agrippina.[7]

The Roman tragic tradition

Virtually all literary forms in use in Rome were borrowed from Greece, and drama, especially tragedy, was no exception. But the Romans were far from embarrassed by the debt; their writers rather made a point of revealing their sources, wherever possible, and of trying to outdo the model, or models, in various ways.

The tradition of performing a Latin drama based upon a Greek original started in the mid-third century BC. The advantage of the practice is clear: the playwright had his script ready to hand and needed only to adapt it for a different sort of audience. But just here there was a problem, at least in the earliest period. Myth, the staple of Greek tragedy, was not so familiar in Rome, and the audience needed some orientation and discreet explication. One early tragedian, Ennius, for example, felt that in the opening lines of his version of Euripides' *Medea* he had to explain that Pelias was a king, that the golden fleece was once on a ram, and that it was to be found in Colchis on the Black Sea; he could not trust his Roman audience to know these details. It has been suggested that this lack of acquaintance with myth, and a sense of its foreignness, may have prevented tragedy from ever having quite the place in the

Roman imagination which it certainly held in Athens, and then in the Greek world more generally.[8] However that may be, the Romans nonetheless produced a tragic literature over about a century and a half, down to the time of Accius, the last professional tragedian in Rome, who died about 90 BC. Thereafter the tradition of tragic drama took a fresh direction, which requires some description.

Down to the time of Accius, and certainly after his death, plays were written and performed for special occasions. Rome, like Athens, had no commercial theatre such as we are used to. Plays were commissioned for performance in a specially constructed theatre (Rome had no permanent stone theatre until 55 BC), and only took place in the context of a religious festival, either at the games in honour of a god, when there were days specially designated for *ludi scaenici* ('theatrical entertainments'), or as part of the celebrations of a triumph or a funeral. But after the time of Accius we first begin to hear of revivals of classic works on the one hand, and on the other adaptations of Greek scripts into Latin by amateur men of letters that were never meant for the sort of performance that has been outlined just now. We begin in other words to detect both a falling off in the production of new scripts for a live stage, and a reliance upon the best of the past for stageworthy vehicles. In addition to revivals we also catch references (already referred to) to the performance of excerpts from classic scripts.[9]

As an example of plays composed with no eye to performance we can point to the four 'translated' by Cicero's brother, Quintus, in sixteen days while he was serving with Julius Caesar in Gaul; his elder brother commends his industry (*Letter to his Brother Quintus* 3.5.7). It may also be significant that Gaius Asinius Pollio, a friend of Virgil and Horace, also wrote tragedies, but there is no reference to their performance (this may be due to poor transmission of information). He may have intended them for private reading, or, more likely, for recitation, a practice he

1. Seneca and Roman Tragedy

is said to have developed in Rome by reading his own works to an invited audience (details of its workings will be given below). Certainly we hear of very few plays that were written with stage-performance in view. One such was famous, the *Thyestes* of Varius Rufus (like Pollio, a friend of Virgil and Horace); this tragedy was performed, perhaps at the triumphal games of Octavian in 29 BC, and was vastly admired. But it is curious and suggestive that Varius, who lived at least another ten years, did not apparently build upon that foundation. The *Thyestes* was his sole dramatic effort, so far as we know. His very much junior contemporary, Ovid, also wrote a tragedy, *Medea*, but he says expressly that it was not designed for the stage (*Tristia* 5.7.27). What was it that drove writers to compose dramas that were not intended for performance outside the salon?

A number of factors are suggested. First, the sheer gigantism of Roman productions: Cicero was disgusted by the tasteless display in a revival of Accius' *Clytemnestra* at the opening of Pompey's theatre in August of 55 BC (*Letters to his Friends* 7.1.2). Props and extras dwarfed any intellectual content a play might have had. Could dialogue be audible over the braying of countless asses? Secondly, newer dramatic forms, the mime and pantomime, especially the latter, were driving the older formal drama into oblivion.[10] The mime was a scripted dramatic action, short and often indecent; women performed (only men appeared in the older tragedies and comedies), and masks were not worn. The rather more serious pantomime was something like the classical ballet of modern times, in that the chief performer danced throughout. Yet the pantomime too was scripted,[11] and an off-stage chorus recited or sang to music the words which the masked dancer interpreted. The plots of pantomimes were more decorous than those of the mime, being based often on older comic or tragic plots; over time however the 'tragic', or at any rate mythical, plot prevailed, and the pantomime must have posed the most serious challenge to the old formal tragedy. The popularity of these two forms weighed heavily with those who commissioned drama for the *ludi scaenici;* they did not have to mount comedies or tragedies, and if the audience wanted something livelier, then that was what it got.

So by the time of Seneca, there was certainly a strong tradition of writing for recitation before a select audience. Goldberg has argued that the move from theatre to recitation hall ensured the survival of tragedy as a living literary form among the élite.[12] The audience at a recitation necessarily focused its attention upon the language, there being no spectacle to distract it. Since the élite's control of language ensured its own position in society and government, tragedy could regain its place as an instrument of political or moral discourse. Arguably then, the change in the character of performance from stage to recitation revitalised and prolonged the tragic tradition at Rome.

It needs however to be said that a play written for recitation is not necessarily unperformable in any other way. Still, a drama freed from the conventions and limitations of actual performance upon a stage can achieve other effects by appealing to the inner eye of the imagination. Here we must take into account the opinion of the educated in antiquity that language alone can vividly conjure up a scene through the power called 'phantasia', visualisation:[13] first, the speaker or writer must 'see' what he is to describe in language, and then he must impose his 'vision' verbally upon his audience. This to be sure is an intellectual's approach; we might recall that Aristotle in his *Poetics* §14, 1453b1-11, had deemed 'opsis', spectacle, the least important aspect of a tragedy, inasmuch as the poet himself, who constructed the plot and composed the words, had little to do with it. Seneca himself was nothing if not an intellectual and may well have subscribed to the notion that 'phantasia' was a pre-eminent literary quality. As an example of this technique of visualisation in our play, we might consider the notorious con-

1. Seneca and Roman Tragedy

clusion, in which Theseus puts together the broken limbs of his son. It might prove laughable in performance, but what counts, as Goldberg has urged,[14] is the father's verbal process of recognition. Here action is secondary, even unnecessary to what can be realised through language alone.

What sort of performance Seneca himself had in mind is still much debated, and it must be clear that we lack the sort of information about performance in his own day that would allow us to say decisively that he intended either recitation or performance or both (or even neither: some think he intended his plays simply to be read in private). It is only fair to lay my own cards on the table and say that I do not believe that Seneca had anything other than recitation in mind, and that there are moreover features of his dramas which would be ludicrous if performed with the means available in his day. Examples will be given when we turn to a critical account of the action of the *Phaedra*. One consideration needs to be emphasised: a play composed for recitation is not somehow inferior as drama. Dylan Thomas' 'Under Milk Wood' is still reckoned a fine piece, but it began life on the radio, and has never been felt to suffer as drama for that. A recitation drama can exploit its differences from one that is to be staged in particular ways; it is, or can be, much freer in its implied movements and in the interaction between characters and audience.[15] It would not diminish Seneca's stature as a dramatist if he had only recitation or reading in view.[16]

2

The Action of the Play

The unfolding of the action

Let us now turn to the play itself and look critically at how Seneca evolves the action.

A hunting party is on the scene; its leader encourages his men to scour Attica (the numerous and recondite place names – Parnes, Thria, Aphidnae, Phyle – make the location clear) for game. At line 54 the speaker prays to Diana, patron goddess of the chase, for success. This he feels assured of and so runs off into the woods (*siluas*, line 82).

A woman is then present on the scene, and obliquely identifies herself as Phaedra (lines 85-91). She deplores the absence of her husband Theseus, on what may prove to be a fatal visit to the Underworld. As if that were not cause enough for grief, she is herself vaguely discontented with her usual activities, and, weirdly, yearns for the hunt (lines 110-11). The real cause of this yearning does not long elude her: she suffers, as the women in her family tend to do, from love for an inappropriate male. Though her speech does not seem to be addressed to anyone in particular, she is attended, as a woman of her status would normally have been, by another female, her Nurse. The Nurse now tries to encourage Phaedra to resist her passion by rehearsing a range of considerations that should deter her. Not least is the somewhat incestuous nature of the attraction (lines 165-77). Phaedra acknowledges the justice of the Nurse's arguments, but says that she is in the grip of madness, *furor* (lines

178, 184), and there is no resisting the madness of love: even the gods succumb to it. The Nurse, something of a rationalist, denounces this doctrine as so much self-delusion and special pleading: only the rich and idle have time to indulge such fancies. The pace of the dialogue now begins to quicken and the women debate in shorter exchanges. Phaedra overrides the Nurse's objections concerning Theseus' probable return and Hippolytus' certain rejection of her attentions. The Nurse then makes a personal appeal (lines 246-9) to which Phaedra rapidly assents, with the grim proviso that since she cannot live with her love she must die (line 254). This was not at all what the Nurse intended and so she now has to plead a new cause, that Phaedra live. In the face of her obstinacy, the Nurse undertakes to approach Hippolytus, a proposal to which Phaedra herself says nothing.

A Chorus of unidentified gender is then present and sings of the power of Love; after listing numerous examples of Love's effects, the Chorus observes that its power sways even a stepmother (lines 356-7). It then asks the Nurse about the course of Phaedra's passion.

At this point we may usefully pause to comment upon how the dramatic action unfolds in a Senecan tragedy. Let us return to what is sometimes called the Prologue, the huntsman's speech and prayer.

What strikes us first of all is that the speaker at no point identifies himself (and no one else present addresses him by name). He simply provides indications of the scene (Attica) and his own activities. Seneca clearly expects a lot of his audience; it somehow knows that the play it is attending – or hearing, or reading – is called *Phaedra*, so a man in that dramatic context who exhibits an interest in hunting, and a devotion to Diana, must be Hippolytus. Seneca feels he does not have to spell this out. Nor does he spell out a central feature of the young man's character, his chastity or aversion to women. This is taken for

2. The Action of the Play

granted by Phaedra and the Nurse (lines 119 and 236-41), but is not so much as hinted at by Hippolytus himself. Now it may be that the hint is in the situation itself: the erotic code (especially in Latin love elegy) had opposed love and hunting (you have to get out of bed early in the morning to hunt), so Hippolytus as hunter may be assumed to be at least uninterested in lovemaking.[1] But in the end Seneca leaves all this at a level of implication, clear enough to the learned audience to which he seems to be appealing. A further point to be made about this scene is that in dramatic terms it accomplishes nothing:[2] the main action is not initiated by Hippolytus' setting off on the hunt (from which, in the way of things, he is bound to return if the dramatic action is to proceed). What the speech achieves is something rather different. In the first place, the hunt covers almost the whole of Attica, and the sweep implied by all the place names suggests heroic activity in a remote, and perhaps to the Roman sensibility, romantic landscape. The speaker's enthusiasm for wild beasts (*ferae*) and woods (*siluae*) is clearly established, and it will be a hallmark of his characterisation later on (see line 718, the last words he utters in the play).[3]

The opening scene between the women would have been slightly unusual on the Greek stage, in that they do not account for their presence 'in the open'. Roman women had greater freedom of movement, so Seneca's characters can dispense with any excuse for being 'out of doors'. Seneca's reliance upon implication is as strong as ever in this scene too, but now he can also forge a thematic link: Phaedra too yearns for wild beasts (line 110), and refers to woods (line 114, 235). This suggests the violation of the wilds by the lover (we note in line 114 *peccare* 'do wrong'): the hunt is to be perverted into an erotic activity, Hippolytus' woodland realm is to be desecrated.[4] Again, this is not said, but might have been implicit to an audience versed in the code of erotic poetry. Seneca, we feel, relies more heavily upon the literary training of his audience than on the straightforward evolution of dramatic action.

This is confirmed too by the use Seneca makes of the Chorus. In the earlier Greek theatre a chorus had physically to move on to the stage, where it tended to stay put throughout the action. Obviously it could not comment upon anything it had not heard or seen for itself. Seneca's Chorus is quite different. There is no reason to suppose it was present when Phaedra revealed her passion for the first time to the Nurse, and yet it clearly knows all about the queen's predicament, and even seems to sympathise, in that it shares the view she propounded that Love is all powerful and irresistible. The Senecan Chorus is thus a commentator rather like the older Greek Chorus, but somehow telepathic in its perceptions. Let us now return to the action.

The Nurse, in answer to the Chorus' request, explains that her mistress is in deep erotic misery. The palace opens (a production technique found on the Greek stage to reveal interior scenes), and we see Phaedra rejecting her usual dress for the outfit of a huntress. (This scene has a decidedly Roman colour: the purple and gold silk, the necklaces and ear-rings of pearl, the perfumed hair – all evoke the elaborate style of the upper-class Roman woman known to Seneca and his audience.) Phaedra is now about to realise her desire to join the chase. At the Nurse's prompting she prays to Diana (woods again – line 410) for help in the seduction of Hippolytus.[5] As if in answer to her prayer, Hippolytus is on the scene (but not expressly from the hunt, lines 424-5), so Phaedra urges the Nurse to perform her earlier undertaking and approach him. (The Nurse's words however suggest that she has forgotten that this initiative was hers.)

Hippolytus enquires after the well-being of the household, and the Nurse, after assuring him that all is well, launches into her appeal. In essence she is trying to bring him round to a sense of the normal, especially what is normal as regards love

2. The Action of the Play

in the young. Love-making and above all reproduction are natural, she urges, and Hippolytus should fall into line with Nature. His reply to this generalised appeal is equally general. He recalls a Golden Age, lived, of course, in the woods (line 485).[6] He rehearses the virtues of that now vanished time, and moves to an account of how sin and crime arose among men (lines 540-58). The end of this part of the harangue is focused upon strife within the family, and women – mothers and stepmothers – as agents of evil. This leads to his main point (lines 559-64): women are the chief source of wickedness. The Nurse now resumes, and the argument becomes a sort of altercation. Hippolytus is obstinate, the Nurse makes no headway. Suddenly, unexpectedly, Phaedra herself comes upon the scene and immediately faints (line 585); Hippolytus takes her in his arms (line 588). Before describing what follows, we may again pause to assess what has unfolded before us.

The opening scene – the Nurse and Phaedra in her chamber – does not in dramatic terms advance the action at all. We already know that Phaedra is distracted by emotion and that she wants to join the chase. The presence of this scene is to be explained by Seneca's adherence to the Roman practice of literary imitation. This in essence was the scene in which Euripides had introduced Phaedra to his audience in the second of his plays on the Hippolytus myth.[7] Seneca wanted to draw upon that famous drama and so borrowed the early scene, not least because it exploited the theme of the hunt. Very adroitly, Seneca gives Phaedra a prayer to Diana, which might seem a sort of perversion of Hippolytus' prayer in the Prologue. He prayed for success in hunting; she prays for success in a sort of hunt too, but now the prey is Hippolytus himself. It may seem odd that such a prayer is directed to Diana, a convinced virgin. Once again, Seneca relies upon subtle thematic links: the Chorus had already reminded the audience that the goddess of the moon herself knew love's pains (lines 309-16). Phaedra therefore does not have to be crudely explicit, she but hints that the goddess has good reason to be an accomplice in securing the favours of a handsome young man (cf. line 422).

We left the action with the entrance of Phaedra, who, on recovering from a faint, sets about presenting her own case in person to Hippolytus. Once she has made herself plain (lines 665, 671), he is duly horrified, and denounces her at length. To ward off her embrace he draws his sword (line 706). When she beseeches him to kill her as a favour, he refuses, so that he will do her no sort of favour at all, and he casts the sword from him (line 714). He feels defiled, and in his last words on the scene he cries out to his ideal place of purity, the woods with their beasts (line 718). The Nurse now stirs herself, and again takes the initiative by urging that Hippolytus must be charged with a criminal act. She summons the citizens of Athens and claims he tried to rape Phaedra; his abandoned sword proves his violence. Phaedra rushes from the scene. The Chorus now sing of Hippolytus' flight, and of his beauty, dangerous in a man. When their song is over, they describe the plotting of the women, who seek to validate their charge against Hippolytus (lines 824-8). Suddenly, and opportunely, Theseus reappears (lines 829-34). Let us again, as usual, scroll back for comment on the second half of the act.

The opening of this scene presents those who believe that the play was to be staged with two problems, at lines 592-9 and 600. At the former point Phaedra, recovering from her faint, is in the arms of Hippolytus, who rushed to assist her when she collapsed. Now unless he is busy chafing her feet, his own head can be no more than about a foot away from hers when she utters an extended aside in which she pretty much gives the game away. Such an aside could be handled quite adroitly on the modern stage, by dimming the lights and focusing a spotlight upon Phaedra – a resource quite lacking to antiquity. It is interesting therefore to note that two dramatists who followed

2. The Action of the Play

Seneca quite closely here altered this business. The sixteenth-century French playwright Robert Garnier (of whom more later) had Phaedra faint, and Hippolytus rush to her aid, but in his version the Nurse prevents Hippolytus from reaching Phaedra, and rouses her mistress herself. Phaedra speaks no aside. This action (Garnier's lines 1309-38) is plausible. Garnier's revision is perhaps unconsciously replicated in the modern Dutch adaptation of the play by the Flemish playwright Hugo Claus: again Hippolytus makes to assist the fallen queen, but Oenone (= the Nurse) prevents him, and again, no aside from Phaedra. This is very telling. Playwrights who keep stage action in view cannot countenance a long, self-revealing aside delivered so close to a listening ear. Unless one is prepared to accept an utterly unrealistic production upon the Roman stage, this present aside strongly suggests either that Seneca was a novice (and *Phaedra* is reckoned an early work), or that he never envisaged the play as performable. The aside becomes an externalisation of an internal thought process. This is just the sort of advantage that a recited play has over an acted one.

The second problem for staging concerns the presence of the Nurse. We must recall that Hippolytus was seen worshipping the statue of Diana alone (line 425). Thus when Phaedra orders the stage to be cleared, there is only one person who can exit: the Nurse. But somehow or other she is back on stage at line 719. That too is problematic because at that point she knows what Phaedra has said to Hippolytus. The only solution is to have her withdraw apparently out of earshot, and yet she must be able to overhear what is said. (D.F. Sutton, *Seneca on the Stage*, p. 51, opts for this fairly clumsy procedure.)

We have already noted Seneca's debt to Euripides. Roman poets sought not just to imitate a model, but to rival and surpass it if possible. In the second half of this act Seneca aims to outdo Euripides. In the analysis which follows it must be made clear that the view set forth is not uncontroversial. While it is obvious that in the extant *Hippolytus* of Euripides, Phaedra and Hippolytus do not meet, I believe that in the earlier of his two Hippolytus plays they also did not deal directly with each other; at any rate there is no clear evidence that they did. My view is that Euripides kept them apart, and perhaps used the Nurse as intermediary, the chief difference being that in the earlier play Phaedra was more prone to accept her passion than in the later one. The author who went one better on this tradition was Ovid, an important literary model for Seneca, to whom he owes much of his poetic diction and expression. In *Heroides* 4 Ovid composed a letter for Phaedra to send Hippolytus; this was boldly innovative,[8] since it brought Phaedra into the realm of the elegiac mistress who, though shying from face-to-face appeal, still operates on her own behalf without a go-between. Seneca resolved to go further than either Euripides or Ovid, and presented us with a woman who could put her own case in the very presence of her beloved.[9]

It has also been observed that the situation Seneca describes reflects the reality of high society in Rome, where well-born *matronae* did not hesitate to take the erotic initiative with men who had caught their fancy. The most notorious example of this in Seneca's own lifetime was the empress Messalina's 'marriage', described by Tacitus in *Annals* 11.31, to the handsomest man in Rome, Gaius Silius. (Silius' fatal good looks became part of the rhetorical tradition, exploited by Juvenal at *Satire* 10.329-45.) If the above reconstruction of the literary tradition is correct, we should see Seneca as a moderniser, bringing the tragic myths up to date wherever Rome provided not dissimilar situations.

Phaedra's deliberated appeal is composed with exceptional tact and sure dramatic development; she works round to her revelation by the adroit use of hint, comparison and allusion. Her cue comes at line 608 when Hippolytus addresses her kindly as 'Mother'. At once she repudiates the name as too

2. The Action of the Play

grand: *matris superbum nomen est et nimium potens* ('the name "mother" is far too exalted and domineering'). She proposes preferable designations: sister, slave even. Now in Latin these words can have erotic overtones, especially the latter which suggests the 'servitude of love' motif, common in erotic poetry. She goes on to emphasise her weakness and dependency, offering him the kingdom. The final two words of her first assault upon him are 'pity a widow' (*miserere uiduae*, line 623). A brief discussion follows about the chances of Theseus' return from the Underworld, and Hippolytus decently says that in his father's absence he will fill his place. He does not understand what meaning Phaedra attaches to that expression (again, in erotic language the place *par excellence* is the bed). In the course of the brief subsequent dialogue Phaedra guardedly expresses her yearnings, and Hippolytus again assumes that she is talking about Theseus (line 645). This is a second cue to Phaedra, and she launches into an appeal which is generally reckoned to be one of the finest pieces of dramatic composition in antiquity. She explains that indeed she is in love with Theseus, as he was when she first saw him, young, strong and handsome: her language is frankly sensuous (lines 651-6), but decent in so far as she is speaking of her husband. She then moves adroitly into a comparison of father and son: Hippolytus blends something stern and fierce with all his father's good looks. She reckons her sister Ariadne would have fallen for him just as she fell for Theseus. At line 666 she makes herself plain: Ariadne fell for Theseus, Phaedra has fallen for Hippolytus. An appeal for sympathy follows, and she concludes her second speech with words that recall the end of the first, 'pity a lover' (*miserere amantis*, line 671). The dramatic power of this whole section of the act is exceptional, and the greatest compliment was paid to it by Racine, who built his whole play *Phèdre* upon the theme of disclosure (more will be said of his debt to Seneca in due course).[10]

Seneca: Phaedra

The Chorus' song is again a development of the preceding action. Phaedra had tactfully expressed her attraction to Hippolytus' features, but the Chorus indulge in an orgy of detail about the charms of masculine good looks. This, however, has some moral purpose: good looks can prove one's undoing. Their warning might have had a particular resonance for a contemporary audience which had fresh in its mind the fate of Silius.

The short descriptive passage at lines 824-8 is puzzling and evokes adverse criticism. What are we to imagine is enacted here? Dumbshow was not a feature of the live stage in antiquity, so how do the Chorus see what they describe? Is it an internal scene, like that adumbrated at lines 384-6? Why, moreover, is Phaedra continuing to present herself as the victim of a rape, hair torn, cheeks streaked with tears? Athens has been alerted already, the sword is proof. Anyway, for whose benefit is the charade being performed? The answer comes quickly enough, with the arrival of Theseus. But that is coincidence, it was not to be predicted. Here we must recall that in the second Hippolytus play of Euripides Theseus was away on a sacred embassy, so his return was imminent. Seneca adopted a different version of the myth (used by Ovid, *Heroides* 4.109-12), his adventure with Pirithous in the Underworld, which, it should be noted, makes Phaedra's sense of abandonment more pathetic. But it does create a small local difficulty in the action, in that we have no idea when he might reappear, if indeed he is ever to do so. But appear he does, and finds his household in confusion (line 850). We return now to the action.

The Nurse comes on scene and explains that Phaedra is determined to die. Theseus insists on speaking to her himself to find out the reason; this she refuses to disclose, until he threatens to torture the Nurse (he just assumes she knows, despite her statement at 860). Phaedra then, on oath, claims to have been raped (though her language is studiedly ambiguous). She refuses to name the culprit (she is either artful or has some

2. The Action of the Play

shame still), and instead shows Theseus the sword, which he recognises. He asks where Hippolytus is, and is told that he has fled (lines 901-2). He then denounces his son unheard (as they do in Italian operas), and with unconscious irony observes that the very beasts do not act in that way (line 913). Hippolytus is to his mind a hypocrite, for all his life in the woods (line 922). Theseus is lashing himself into a fury. He promises to follow the fugitive to any place of refuge he may seek, however remote. Suppose he cannot track him down? In that case, he has a resource, a curse which his true father Neptune will fulfil. In lines 945-58 he utters the irreversible prayer: let Hippolytus live no more!

The Chorus now sing of the mutability of Fortune, and the powerlessness of virtue to defeat vice. After this short song is over, they mark the arrival of a new character, who turns out to be a Messenger.

At Theseus' request he relates the manner of Hippolytus' death. It is clear that Neptune heard and answered the father's prayer, and sent a bull from the sea which terrified Hippolytus' horses as he drove along the beach on his way to exile. The horses bolted and fled inland, dragging their driver behind them. His body thus became horribly mangled and indeed he was torn limb from limb (Hippolytus has what is called a 'speaking name' since it is formed from two Greek words that combined mean 'torn apart by horses') before his torso was spitted on a tree trunk. The Messenger concludes by observing that his servants are trying to find all the portions of the body for burial (lines 1105-14). Theseus is moved as a father in spite of himself, and the Messenger reproves him for the apparent hypocrisy.[11]

The Chorus again sing of the changeability of Fortune, and again at the end of the song announce the arrival of a character on the scene. It is Phaedra, who has somehow got wind of Hippolytus' death. She is distraught at what her lie has

29

Seneca: Phaedra

achieved, and she reveals the truth. That done, she kills herself with a sword (of unspecified provenance). Theseus naturally blames his haste in cursing his son; he finds himself a criminal once more, and even seems to be contemplating suicide. The Chorus reminds him that he has a duty to bury his son (line 1245). To do so he must first piece the body together again. In vain! Not all the parts are to hand, so for the time being burial must be partial, and the rest of his son's remains are to be sought (lines 1278-9). His final words parody tomb inscriptions, in a wish that earth may lie heavy on Phaedra.

The action just described unfolded straightforwardly for the most part: the charge against Hippolytus, the fury and curse of Theseus, the Messenger's account, and the final scene all follow one from the other without difficulty. But Seneca has provided critics of his stageworthiness with some grist to their mill, chiefly in the final act, where the text presents would-be producers with one serious problem, and a minor one. The minor one relates to Hippolytus' sword. It is one of the great pities that Seneca failed to make explicit in his script that the sword with which Phaedra kills herself was Hippolytus'. That may seem a fair guess (and is assumed by many commentators), but once again we are up against a problem of staging. Theseus ought to have the sword in his own hands at lines 898-900, so that he can inspect the tell-tale device of ownership. What happens to it then? Does he give it back to Phaedra, and if so, why? Since he does not (necessarily) leave the stage after his return from the Underworld, it might be supposed that he keeps the sword for the rest of the play (he could hand it to an attendant). Perhaps then that is why the sword in Phaedra's hand is not expressly identified by her as belonging to Hippolytus: it isn't his. This does not really diminish the symbolism of the scene in which Phaedra kills herself, but the common (mis)identification of her sword as Hippolytus' should be dropped.

The second, and really serious, problem is thrown up by line

2. *The Action of the Play*

1158, in which Theseus asks explicitly why Phaedra laments over the hated body of Hippolytus. Indeed she does go on to address the mangled remains which presumably lie before her in lines 1168-9. But it is only much later at line 1247 that Theseus, reminded of his duty by the Chorus, bids them carry the remains of his son's body on to the stage. Producers who respect the text can only do one thing, and have servants bring some parts of the body on to the stage before Phaedra appears. Some modern translations with stage directions suggest such an action at about line 1109 during the Messenger's speech, but the Latin itself does not support this. Sutton suggests that servants with some of the remains enter with Theseus at the beginning of the act; but he has overlooked his own supposition, based upon the implicit directions, that Theseus never left the stage.[12] As he admits, the early arrival of the remains, to account for Phaedra's lament, causes them to lie neglected for some time, until the Chorus reminds Theseus of their presence, an implausible situation. On any account, if Seneca intended in a performance the early arrival of the limbs, he broke radically with the ancient convention that stage action had to be generated from what people actually say. This would be an anomalous situation indeed, and convinces some that such a case as this demonstrates that Seneca did not have staging in mind.

Phaedra's suicide on stage is a characteristically Senecan piece of action (lines 1197-8). The Athenian stage knew few killings in front of the audience (Sophocles' *Ajax* was one), and Horace had therefore laid it down as an invariable law that such things happened offstage (*Art of Poetry* 185 'Medea shouldn't kill her children in public' – in Seneca's version of course she does just that). Death on stage may in fact have been commoner than our extant Greek scripts suggest, and it may have become a more acceptable practice in later drama. At any rate, Senecan characters kill or commit suicide quite often on stage, and we should probably regard this as evidence for a certain grossness

Seneca: Phaedra

of sensibility in the Roman audience (even one at a recitation), a grossness encouraged by what they encountered in the amphitheatre. Death as spectacle was a Roman pastime, and even though Seneca himself deplored it in an eloquent letter (number 7 in the *Letters* to Lucilius), he was to some extent infected by the taste.

The re-assembly of Hippolytus' body at the end of the play is often faulted, but it shows Seneca yet once more drawing upon the rich reserves of Athenian tragedy. A similar scene had concluded Euripides' *Bacchae*, in which Agave put back together the broken limbs of her son Pentheus (this portion of the play is now lost but the scene is well attested). That said, imitation is not in itself a guarantee of literary or dramatic fitness. What was probably very moving in Euripides is generally deemed laughable in Seneca. But if, as was urged above, the final scene is meant not to be seen but imagined, then much of the objection evaporates.

The role of the Chorus

It may be appropriate at this point, after the critical analysis of the action of the play, to say something about the use made of the Chorus. Clearly it is very different in a Senecan drama from what it was expected to do in an Athenian drama; that in itself is no fault. Horace, again, legislated that the Chorus should play its part, just like any other character, and that its songs should suit the action (*Art of Poetry* 193-201). Perhaps his insistence upon the last point shows – what we seem to detect in some of the late plays of Euripides – a weakening of the once intimate relation between the Chorus and the other actors. That weakening may have been further developed in subsequent drama; we cannot be sure. What is clear however is that the Senecan Chorus is almost entirely divorced from the action. Our play is something of an exception in that the Chorus regularly (as was

2. The Action of the Play

noted in the analysis above) announces the arrival of a character, a traditional function (see lines 829-34, 989-90, 1154-5), or speaks with one (lines 338-9); they also take note in their song of the flight of Hippolytus (line 736). More traditionally still they comment critically upon the action (lines 824-8: a problem passage however), and tell Theseus what to do at lines 1244-6 (but probably not at lines 1256-61). Their role is thus in the *Phaedra* functional to a degree not found in some of the other plays (perhaps another sign that this is an early essay in the genre). But there is also a good measure of untraditional use made of the Chorus.

As was noted in the analysis, their arrival or presence on the scene is odd, in that they are fully equipped with a knowledge of Phaedra's condition, even though she has only just revealed it to the Nurse. Furthermore, in their first song (lines 274-357) they seem to support her view that love is an irresistible force; that binds them to some degree into the drama, as does their reference to the love of stepmothers (lines 356-7).[13] Their second song, likewise, on the dangers to which his beauty has exposed Hippolytus, keeps them abreast of the action. But with the third song (lines 959-88) their involvement becomes looser as they sing on one of the tritest themes in Senecan tragedy, the mutability of Fortune. It is trite, because all tragedy turns upon a change in fortune, from good to bad. There is still a tenuous link with the action, in that they draw attention to the snares of lust (line 981) and to trickery (line 982), but since these references are lumped together with other sins and misfortunes they do not exactly stand out as important themes of the ode. Again, their final song (lines 1123-53) has a traditional and general theme, the wheel of Fortune; this they do relate to the disaster which Theseus has brought upon his household (lines 1144-8), though their reference is curiously low-key. Their concluding observation, that the account with the Underworld is settled, now that Hippolytus has replaced the absconded Theseus, is equally cool. On balance then, this Chorus keeps a pretty close eye upon the action and offers its (usually distant) assessment of what it has seen. Only the third ode could have occurred in any other play.

The Chorus then has a role to play, but why it sings when it does, and whether or not it is always present, is less clear. The Chorus in a Greek play helped to articulate the action, whereas Seneca uses it chiefly to punctuate his acts. On the whole he wants to keep to a five act structure, and it is the song of the Chorus which indicates the break between acts. At line 273 it is pretty clear that Phaedra and the Nurse *exeunt*; a bare stage is naturally filled by the entering Chorus (though they do not explain why they have decided to appear). Likewise at line 735 the main characters presumably leave the stage, the Chorus' cue to sing. It is the next act that causes dramatic trouble, and needs careful production. The Chorus are aware of the women's fraud, they say so explicitly at line 828. So, if present in the next act, why do they not speak out when Phaedra falsely accuses Hippolytus of rape? (On the Athenian stage such silence had to be secured by getting the Chorus to swear an oath, which they honoured however reluctantly.) Is the vague generality of their subsequent song a hint that they have not been present at the just completed scene? If not present, why do they 're-enter' just after Theseus has cursed his son? Their final song is, dramatically considered, unnecessary: Theseus stays on stage after the presumed departure of the Messenger, so all that was needed was an announcement of Phaedra's cry and re-appearance with a sword. Here above all we see the use of the Chorus for purposes of punctuation; Seneca wants a pause between the scene with the Messenger and the finale. The Chorus have nothing particular to say, and so get it over with briskly.

The Chorus presented Seneca with dramatic difficulties, which he did not always sort out very adroitly (it is worth noting that the unknown author of the *Octavia* made a decent attempt

2. The Action of the Play

to integrate his double chorus into the action). We have, moreover, a possible glimpse into his method of composition in the fragmentary *Phoenician Women*; all that has been transmitted to us of that play is dialogue, and the most plausible account for its condition is that the play was unfinished, and published after the writer's death in a collected edition of his dramas. If that account is correct, it shows that Seneca composed his dialogue portions first, and slotted in the choral odes only after completing the spoken parts of the drama. If there was no dramatic reason for an ode then he simply inserted one to mark the departure of one character and the arrival of another – though that in itself did not require a choral interlude, as we see from the hectic last act of his *Agamemnon*. The fact is that the Chorus was still felt to be an essential feature in tragedy, as it no longer was in comedy; in Athens the commission to compose a tragedy for the public festivals had actually been called the award of a chorus. So a Chorus there still had to be for the sake of the genre, even when it had ceased to perform a substantial role in the action. Seneca was not prepared to innovate and dispense with it altogether (unless, as some maintain, the *Phoenician Women*, described above, is just such an experimental tragedy of pure dialogue without choral songs), but on the other hand he did not take much trouble to revitalise its role as an active character in the drama.

3

The Major Themes of the Play

In the course of the critical analysis of the action a number of the play's dominant themes were necessarily referred to. It is now time to draw fuller attention to them.

Nature[1]

Seneca, as a Stoic, endorsed one of that school's chief doctrines, that life should be lived in accordance with nature. But what does that entail? It should be clear from the critical analysis of the play that there exist alternative models, and Seneca may have been attracted to drama (or to this dramatic situation) for the opportunity it offered to set rival views into opposition.

We encounter nature in its most obvious form in the Prologue, Hippolytus' summons to the hunt. As was noted in the analysis above, the emphasis there is not on his chastity (a character trait), but on the wilds and their denizens, the beasts. That too is perhaps why Seneca reversed the opening situation found in the second Euripidean *Hippolytus*, in which the young man returns from the hunt: Seneca wants us to see him rather setting off joyfully into his ideal realm. This note is sustained when Phaedra discloses her desire to hunt, but she sees the woods, in the light of her family history, as a place of sin (line 114). Hippolytus has never thought of that! So we are faced with a dilemma: is the life of the woods an ideal or a snare?

Seneca: Phaedra

When the Chorus sing their first ode, they draw attention to the power of sex among the beasts (lines 339-50), and significantly refer to the woods echoing with the lovesick lion's roar (line 350). Perhaps after all, Hippolytus' chosen world is not free of the impulse he despises. This hint is further developed in Phaedra's almost sacrilegious prayer to Diana; the goddess is at once located amid woods and groves (line 409) by her supplicant, who however reminds the maiden tactfully of her own erotic leanings (line 422).

The norm which Nature establishes is also developed in the Nurse's appeal to Phaedra (lines 165-77), especially at lines 173 and 176, where she draws attention to the overthrow of Nature's sexual boundaries within the family: she warns Phaedra against incest. This point is taken up by Theseus who contrasts the natural avoidance of incest among animals with the alleged rape by Hippolytus (lines 913-14).[2]

The issue comes to a head in the exchange between the Nurse and Hippolytus. In her appeal the Nurse says explicitly at line 481, in conclusion to her argument as a whole, that the young man should follow nature as his guide in life. Superficially considered, her injunction fairly follows from what she has said. She used two arguments, that a young man should enjoy his youth, and that procreation is necessary. These she validated by appeal to divine ordinance (lines 451 and 466). She further strengthened her case by drawing attention to the procreative impulse of wild things (lines 472-4), an impulse found in Hippolytus' own favourite haunt the woods, with their beasts (*derit ... siluis fera*, 'the forests will lack beasts', 473). Thus on her view Nature enjoins pleasure at the appropriate time and sexual activity. Her case cannot be faulted, either in Stoic or in 'Hippolytean' terms (though of course her real purpose is perverted). Everything has built up to this, that the woods are full of procreating creatures.

Hippolytus' reply is curious, because it does not address the

3. The Major Themes of the Play

issue of natural behaviour head-on. Hippolytus has a model of social development founded upon the notion of gradual moral decay. In a now long-vanished Golden Age mankind loved the woods (line 485), and led a blameless life amid them, where he hunted the wild beasts (his only use of guile, line 502). The trees of the woods provided food too (lines 515 and 538), simple but wholesome. Decay, in his view, began with wealth, and soon trees provided branches as weapons (line 545). Wild nature has been put to bad use by subsequent ages. He never develops this as regards sexuality, but simply denounces womankind as the chief of all evils. His justification of his point of view at line 567 is odd, since it jumbles reason, nature, and 'fatal passion'. In effect he cannot answer the Nurse's argument; his attachment to his ideal is what we would call romantic, and like romantic attachments in literature generally, it will prove deadly. There is no resolution between the alternative models of what is natural behaviour. Hippolytus can only appeal, in what is surely one of the most affecting moments in the play, to his lost realm of woods and beasts in the last words we hear him utter in his blank despair at Phaedra's attempt to seduce him (line 718).

Family values

Crime, like accidents, occurs chiefly in the home, a situation which developed after the Golden Age, as Hippolytus himself observed (lines 553-8). *Phaedra* exposes a particular sin within the family that is still strongly tabooed: incest.[3] Indeed, so deep-rooted was the taboo at Rome that no Latin dramatist of the early period had put the myth of Phaedra (or of Oedipus, for that matter) on to the stage, since the prospect of incest between stepson and stepmother (or between mother and son) was an unacceptable topic in that moral frostpocket, Republican Rome. With the empire, and the retreat of drama from the public stage to the salon, however, such restraint was no longer necessary.

Seneca: Phaedra

Seneca seems to have gone out of his way on no fewer than three occasions to retrieve tragic myths neglected by his predecessors.[4] These particular tales (and their famous Greek models) acted perhaps more directly upon Seneca's imagination than some of the other stories he appropriated. The social climate of the day may well have provided some encouragement. Caligula, for instance, was thought to have had an incestuous relation with his sister, and Claudius' marriage to Agrippina was theoretically incestuous, since she was his niece (incest was technically circumvented by having her adopted outside his own family). Whatever lay behind the choice of myth, Seneca exploits in this play the themes of an inherited disposition to wrong-doing and the transgression of the boundaries of relationship. What is often seen to explain the cycle of wrongdoing in which the characters are implicated is the doom of heredity.[5] Now here a strong native element enters into Seneca's characterisation, for the Romans believed in inherited character traits: you behave as you do because you belong to a certain family (for example, the Claudii were notorious for pride, according to Tacitus, *Annals* 1.4.3).

Phaedra shares this attitude to family traits, and finds in herself a predisposition to unnatural love thanks to her mother, Pasiphae, who was punished by Venus with the love of a bull (line 113).[6] Pasiphae passed on her lustful character to her daughters, for Ariadne, Phaedra's sister, also committed crime, by helping her lover Theseus kill her half-brother, the Minotaur. Hence Phaedra regards her lineage as accursed (lines 126-8), and she claims to be unable to avoid the inherited evil, a stand which the Nurse tries to oppose (lines 142-4). She points out to Phaedra that her mother Pasiphae is a warning example, and that she should not produce some monstrous offspring by sleeping with both father and son (lines 170-2). Phaedra also looks at her situation from another family angle at lines 665-6, when she says that the males in Theseus' family have seduced the

3. The Major Themes of the Play

females of her own: Theseus led Ariadne astray, and now his son Hippolytus is attracting Phaedra. Once Phaedra has revealed her love to Hippolytus, he denounces her as a true daughter of Pasiphae, only rather worse (lines 688-9).

Hippolytus too is seen as the product of his ancestry; according to the Nurse (line 232), his avoidance of marriage demonstrates the Amazonian strain in his make-up (his mother, Antiope, was an Amazon). Genetic inheritance can however be turned against him, and he is exposed to the charge of inherited vice. When Theseus is told of the alleged rape, he mistakenly recognises in his son the promiscuity of the Amazons (lines 907-11: traditionally they would go out to mate with any man, simply to secure female offspring – males they killed).[7]

It should however be emphasised that as a Stoic Seneca had no truck with this notion of inherited propensity to sin, and he expressly denounces it in Letter 94.55-6: 'it is wrong to think our faults are innate; they come later and are adopted ... Nature begot us unblemished and free.' It is therefore remarkable that he does not have his Chorus enunciate this doctrine to set the moral record straight.

A notion related to hereditary guilt is that people behave, as it were, 'true to form'. Theseus is not regarded as having inherited his character, but he shows a propensity for violence against his kin. He killed Hippolytus' mother (lines 227, 927 and 1167); it is perhaps significant that Seneca alone of those who refer to that liaison calls Antiope Theseus' wife (line 226), stressing the validity of their bond and the legitimacy of their son Hippolytus (line 1112).[8] That makes Theseus' crime the more wicked. Phaedra charges him with always being the bane of his relations, in that he caused the death of his foster-father Aegeus (line 1165-6) as well as of Hippolytus.

This theme is sharpened at the verbal level by the frequent juxtaposition of words for family members (a feature of the Latin that is not always easy to reproduce in translation) for example, line 555 'by brother a brother slain, by hand of a son a father'.[9] This feature is given a special twist at lines 1199-1200 when Theseus says that he must learn from a stepmother what he as a father owes his slain son. Now the stepmother is traditionally hateful towards her stepchildren, and one of the most frequent rhetorical points made in the drama is that the love Phaedra feels for Hippolytus is somehow additionally 'unnatural', since as his stepmother she should dislike him (see lines 356-7, the last of the first choral ode, and 638).

Seneca shows great finesse in his use of this motif in the scene in which Phaedra reveals her passion to Hippolytus. At line 608 he addresses her politely as 'Mother', in urging her to explain to him her concerns. She at once takes the cue: 'mother' is too proud a name, she would rather be called his sister or his slave (both words, as mentioned above, could have erotic overtones in Latin, given an appropriate context). She calls him 'Hippolytus' three times, rather than 'son', and at the end of her first speech refers to herself as a widow, presuming Theseus gone for good (line 624). Hippolytus demurs but assures her that until his father returns he will 'fill his father's place' (line 633), an ambiguous remark which seems to tally with Phaedra's own redistribution of family roles. The tragic misfortunes which afflict households are sharpened by this regular employment of the terms of family relationship.

Furor vs *ratio*

Madness, *furor*, is one of the recurrent themes of Senecan tragedy generally.[10] This madness is not the mental incapacity to conduct oneself normally in life, but rather any yielding to an irrational impulse, usually in tragedy to excess. The Stoics in fact preached a paradoxical doctrine, to the effect that all men are mad (save the Stoic sage), inasmuch as they all give in to the passions of greed, envy, lust, etc., rather than heed the

3. The Major Themes of the Play

corrective voice of reason (*ratio*). Seneca's dramas often realise this conflict between madness and reason. In *Phaedra furor* drives all the main characters, not only the queen, but Hippolytus and Theseus as well.

Phaedra acknowledges at the outset that her desire to cherish the woods is 'raving' (*furens*, line 112). That word quickly acquires specific colour in the context: this is clearly the madness of love, a connotation common to the Latin words *furor* and *insania*. After the Nurse has attempted to dissuade her, Phaedra objects that *furor* compels her to wickedness (line 178). It is at this point that she brings into play the notion of rational action: her mind (*animus*) acts knowingly (*sciens*), but it cannot strive to effect sensible plans (*sana consilia*; lines 179-80). This is not a particularly Stoic observation; Ovid had encapsulated a similar moral quandary in describing Medea, who sees and approves the better course of action but follows the worse (*uideo meliora proboque, deteriora sequor, Metamorphoses* 7.20). Phaedra asserts that *furor* is now in charge of her (line 184), and she even goes on to call it divine (a plausible identification, given that she is referring to love). This line of argument the Nurse expressly repudiates at line 197, again using the key-word, *furor*. She begs Phaedra to put a stop to her madness (*furorem*, line 248). Paradoxically, once the queen agrees to do this, but realises that only death will ensure her chastity, the Nurse regards that line of action too as an instance of 'madness' (*mentis effrenae impetus*, 'the impulse of an unchecked mind', line 255), and comes down in favour of the madness of love (line 268). Phaedra seems unable to escape madness of some sort! The Nurse is surely right to ascribe to erotic *furor* Phaedra's irruption onto the stage to confront Hippolytus in person with her love (line 584). When her passion is rejected by Hippolytus, who then threatens her with death, she claims that he is curing her of her madness (*sanas furentem*, line 711). That however is premature: she has one mad act left to perform. She attributes

Seneca: Phaedra

to madness (*demens*, line 1193) her decision to blame Hippolytus for rape. When she re-appears in the last scene, determined to commit suicide Theseus regards it as a mad impulse (line 1156), but Phaedra gives a rather different account of herself. Now she is rational, it seems, and feels bound to pay an equivalent penalty, death for death. At the end *ratio*, which in Latin means not just 'reason', but 'account', has balanced the accounts between stepmother and stepson.

Phaedra however is not alone in her 'madness'. She identifies Theseus' visit to the Underworld with his friend Pirithous as a token of his *furor* (line 96). For his part, when Theseus is told that Hippolytus has raped Phaedra, he claims to recognise in his son the innate erotic *furor* of the Amazons (line 909). Hippolytus when trying to account for his loathing of women says inconclusively at line 566 that his resolution can be ascribed to reason, nature, or fatal madness. The run of the line suggests that it is the last term which truly identifies his disposition. So up to a point all the characters, in conformity with Stoic teaching, display (or are assumed to display) a sort of madness, against which reason mounts only the feeblest defence.

Madness even spreads to the beasts and the elements (though they both lack reason). The Chorus remarks upon the erotic *furor* of bucks (line 344), and the sea is called raving (*insani*, line 351). Not surprisingly, the bull which Theseus' curse summons from the sea drives Hippolytus' horses mad (line 1070). In the end, nothing in this play is immune from madness.

The moral world of the play

The moral world of Senecan drama is something of a wasteland, surprisingly not dissimilar from that moral desert found in the comic novel of his contemporary, Petronius. The same elements of deception and violence, unreason, and, on the intrapersonal

3. The Major Themes of the Play

level, rejection and failure darken the atmosphere without relief.

A conspicuous feature of this play which contributes strongly to our sense of moral misdirection is the absence of any management of the action by higher powers (though the Chorus for their part often lay misfortune at the door of chance or of fate). Again, at least one of Seneca's contemporaries shared that attitude, his nephew Lucan. In his epic poem, *De bello ciuili* (*The Civil War*), on the civil war fought out between Julius Caesar and Pompey the Great in the early 40s BC, he dismantled something of the traditional epic machinery by excluding direct divine intervention in the action. Seneca may have had a personal motive for leaving the gods out of his tragedies, since as a Stoic he does not like to conceive of divinity, the agent of providence, as acting against human well-being. (Even the angry Juno of *Hercules Furens* (*Hercules Insane*) acts to check the hero's presumed over-ambition (lines 65 and 74); she is not the spiteful antagonist that she appears to be in Virgil's *Aeneid*.) The lack of the divine oversight makes the drama's morality especially bleak, since human suffering is here unvalidated by heaven. What makes this the more impressive is Seneca's reliance upon our recollection of the tragic situation as imagined by Euripides, who set the whole action within a divine framework, the rivalry between Aphrodite and Artemis.[11]

Let us first consider the case of Hippolytus, who in both versions of his myth dies. As Euripides sets out his tragedy, he arguably deserves some sort of punishment or reproof, since he has wittingly defied a powerful god, Aphrodite, and is warned of the dangers of his intransigence early in the play by an old servant. Aphrodite, moreover, says she is punishing him for his errors. In Seneca's version, Hippolytus' death is not a divine punishment, and so it seems completely undeserved: it is sheer bad luck. Euripides moreover softened the blow by having Artemis appear to her devotee in the final scene and promise (i) to take revenge upon a favourite of Aphrodite's (Actaeon, who will die while hunting), and (ii) to create a cult in Hippolytus' honour. Moreover, she sees to it that the son is reconciled with his father, Theseus. Seneca, by dispensing with the gods, offers no compensation to Hippolytus of any sort, and, by having Hippolytus die off-stage, he renders Theseus incapable of making any amends for his misdirected curse; he is left a ruined man.

Phaedra too becomes a different sort of agent in a play without divine antagonists. Euripides' Phaedra commits suicide without knowing how her charge against Hippolytus will affect him; she has simply to account for her death, to protect her own reputation, and to secure the well-being of her children. Quite unwittingly she plays into Aphrodite's hands. Seneca's Phaedra is no one's accomplice or cat's paw. She incriminates Hippolytus deliberately, and dies in the full knowledge of her own wickedness in compassing the death of an innocent man, a deed for which she cannot be forgiven.

Thus Seneca is, unexpectedly for a Stoic, the complete realist: on his telling of the myth, there is no divine scheme which sets the agenda for the human actors. Everyone in this play acts as they choose to; passion overwhelms reason, but the passion is not imposed or directed from above. So the human soul is not besieged by some external enemy, rather it becomes the battleground of an internal, civil war. The characters work against themselves and each other, but not against a god. This is in effect a new kind of tragedy, operating upon a purely human plane.

Phaedra's love offers an exemplary case. In Euripides she is a victim of Aphrodite.[12] We find this victimisation hard to countenance, but there is still a privilege in having a god pitted against one – this applies to Hippolytus as well: it matters terribly to Aphrodite that he should not succeed in defying her, so that his virginity becomes significant: he is not a harmless

3. The Major Themes of the Play

Orphic crank, but a serious threat to the goddess' authority. Nor is Phaedra's love the refuge of a neglected wife. She does not want what happens to her, but her irresistible condition has come from a god, and, as Euripides ensures that we shall know, it is part of a plan (of revenge), something we can understand (if not exactly assent to). But Seneca's Phaedra is apparently all on her own. She says that the love which afflicts her comes from a vengeful goddess (lines 124-8), but that we may regard as a strategy for dignifying in her own eyes a disgraceful lust, and the Nurse makes just this point at lines 195-8. We have not actually seen the goddess set this trap, as we do in Euripides.

Hippolytus' virginity, taking the form of a proud devotion to Artemis, became impossible in a god-free world, as Seneca astutely recognised. Euripides took it seriously because it was a form of self-commitment to a divinity, Artemis; hunting – association with the beasts in the wild – was the young man's communion with his god (this is a commonly held view in ancient and other societies with regard to male virginity; we may compare Enkidu in the *Epic of Gilgamesh*). That communion we actually see represented on the stage when Artemis takes her heartbreaking farewell of her devotee in the final scene. But Seneca has removed the gods, and so his Hippolytus can no longer account for his continued celibacy on grounds of religious devotion. When he describes his preference for the wild woods, it is purely in terms of the moral innocence of the life lived there (lines 483-558); at no point does he suggest that he is personally closer to any god in the forests, though significantly he claims that he can well believe primitive man, who did mix with the gods, lived first in the woods (lines 525-7). That is clearly not the case nowadays. At this point however Seneca does in my view fail somewhat in imagination: when his Hippolytus turns to explain why he wants to avoid women (lines 559-64) he comes across as no more than a traditional misogynist (or worse: it has been suggested that he represents a repressed homosexual – a very modern concept). He cannot claim a positive devotion to a chaste ideal, as represented in the goddess of the hunt, the mistress of the beasts. His hunt associated him to be sure with Diana (see lines 54-84, 424), but chastity was not the basis of their relation.

As was suggested above, this elision of the gods may have something to do with Seneca's own Stoicism, which denied that the gods were direct agents of human misfortune, except as a sort of test of moral fibre (we emerge from suffering as better people). His moral world is therefore wholly human; the gods are appealed to, and their workings are sometimes presupposed by the actors, but they cannot be sure. With one exception: Theseus' curse (lines 941-58) is executed by his father Neptune. Yet this too fits into the bleak world of morality in Seneca's dramas. He was not alone in suggesting that what did move the gods to act was only a desire to avenge. Lucan too says as much when he reflects in his own voice as narrator upon the action, and wishes that the gods had been as keen to guard Roman freedom as they clearly were to punish its destroyers:

> *felix Roma quidem ciuisque habitura beatos*
> *si libertatis superis tam cura placeret*
> *quam uindicta placet.*

> 'Happy indeed were Rome, and sure to have happy citizens, if the gods cared as much to ensure her freedom as they do to avenge its loss.'
> *De bello ciuili* 4.807-9

The same 'theodicy' is found in Tacitus, where he (certainly borrowing Lucan's idea) claims that the horrors of the civil wars following upon the suicide of Nero proved that that gods were not concerned so much to preserve Rome's well-being, as to punish those who did her wrong (*adprobatum est non esse curae*

3. The Major Themes of the Play

deis securitatem nostram, esse ultionem, 'it was demonstrated that the gods cared less for our tranquillity than for our punishment'; *Histories* 1.3.2). Yet Lucan and Tacitus still seem to feel that the gods punish the deserving at any rate; they are only sorry that punishment does not precede the crime, to save Rome from civil war. Seneca's world of myth is altogether bleaker, since vengeance there falls on an innocent man and the god who destroys him is no free agent. Neptune is bound to fulfil the wishes of his son (as Theseus reminds him at line 953), even if, as we might speculate, he could know, as a god, how unhappy the event would prove. The human being, Theseus, is the real agent of vengeance (he admits it at line 1210), the god is merely his tool (cf. line 1206: *irae facilis assensor meae* 'who too readily assent to my rage'), and acts only to harm. So after all even this one intervention of a divinity does not upset the overall picture of a moral world in which human agents alone operate, engineering their own and each other's misery.

4

Characterisation

The individuals

From the point of view of the discussion of the leading themes in the drama it might be deduced that readers tend to believe that Seneca's characters embody and instantiate his ethical concepts rather than exercise the sort of individualism that we are used to in other dramatic traditions. Comparing his characterisation to that of Euripides is useful up to a point, but we must always bear in mind the different dramatic tradition in which he worked, and Seneca's own possible aims.

Phaedra is the focus of his attention, and the play is rightly named after her. Before looking more closely at her characterisation we should bear in mind the belief prevalent among Roman men that females are irrational, that is to say, they are in thrall to their emotions and passions, and naturally more lustful than men. Seneca himself, for instance, says that woman is a 'thoughtless creature, unrestrained in pursuit of its desires' ('imprudens animal ... cupiditatum incontinens', *Dialogue* 2.14.1),[1] a notion found in the poets, for example, Propertius 3.19 and Ovid, *Art of Love* 1.281-2. His portrayal of Phaedra fits this characterisation. She rejects the Nurse's attempt to impose reasonable restraint, even though she acknowledges its sense (lines 177-80). She is thus the embodiment of irrational erotic passion. She brings considerable self-awareness however to bear upon the analysis of her situation, and Seneca's treatment is rightly regarded as realistic. She tries to ascribe her yearning to fate, and when the Nurse condemns it as mere lust, she makes a heroic resolve to overcome it and restore her modesty (*pudor*) by committing suicide.

In the Second Act, however, she is altogether more passive, in the grip of her desire to be with Hippolytus. She shows mental irresolution and physical debility, as if she were degenerating before our eyes. This change in characterisation has been criticised. W.S. Barrett has described Phaedra's lapse from determination into a neurotic as inept.[2] We might prefer to credit Seneca with a valid insight into the inconsistency of the human heart. Her earlier resolve is being eroded by anxiety, but she will recover it. Her personal approach to Hippolytus is amazing. As has been suggested already, Seneca was arguably the first to depict such a scene (i.e. without the use of a go-between), and he has risen to the challenge impressively. Phaedra's circumspect ensnaring of the young man is plausibly evolved, and there is no shirking the physicality of her attraction to the boy. She frankly admits that in Hippolytus she loves the young Theseus, with his wisp of beard, his lovely complexion, and the soft skin over his muscles (lines 646-54). Not much is left to the imagination here! Realism is again dominant. But the picture acquires yet darker colours. That was the young Theseus: Hippolytus himself adds something, a rough quality, inherited from his Amazon mother. Phaedra is drawn to the combination of handsome boy and brusque manner. We are dealing here with quite subtle observation of the dynamics of erotic attraction.

Our assessment of Seneca's characterisation of Phaedra must depend to some degree upon the issue of staging the drama. At a recitation the presence of characters is not necessarily much of an issue: if they are not speaking or being spoken too, then they are not exactly 'present'. But in a staged version presence is apparent. The Third Act complicates the character of Phaedra if she is on stage the whole time. The point is that

4. Characterisation

once she has denounced Hippolytus as a rapist (and it is perhaps significant of her recklessness that she makes the denunciation herself rather than leaving the job to the Nurse), we naturally condemn her as a liar. But does she also unflinchingly hear Theseus curse his son? Boyle, in his edition, for instance, leaves Phaedra on stage for the denunciation. How then does a spectator regard her? As a monster of indifference? She might of course be instructed by a producer to make gestures of dismay (in antiquity the mask would have concealed any facial expression), but one might still legitimately wonder why she makes no verbal reaction to the outcome of her charge. I therefore suggested in my commentary that in a staged production she should exit with the Nurse after line 902. But there is no indication of that in the text, and this play, as has been noted already, is rich in cues for entrance and exit. We are left with something of a dilemma in this act, and indeed in the next too, if Phaedra is left on stage for most of the Messenger's account of the death of Hippolytus; this was apparently done in the Exeter University production described by Fortey and Glucker. In their staging she exits at line 1104. But we are still faced with the problem of reaction. Nothing in the text suggests a response on her part to the narrative, in all its horror, of the innocent young man's death. Once again, she can only seem unmoved if she does nothing in dumbshow, but if she does anything it is odd that neither Theseus nor the Messenger take note of it. Staging, after all, still has its problems, and they impact upon the assessment of character.

In the final act Phaedra reverts to her intention formed in the first act of committing suicide. But now she has an additional reason: she must atone to Hippolytus for what she has done to him, and so recover some of her lost self-respect. She publicly vindicates the innocence of Hippolytus and condemns herself (lines 1191-8). (We might at this point contrast the behaviour of Racine's Phèdre, who puts a lot of the blame on her old nurse Oenone. Seneca's Phaedra is no shirker.) Once again she wants to follow him, but not now in the erotic sense (contrast lines 1179-80 with 233-5): she comes as a sacrifice to the dead, *inferiae* (line 1198). The economy and realism of this scene are impressive. Emotion and intellect have fought out their battle in Phaedra, and it seems that in the end reason has recovered its sway. She confesses and tries to atone; more in purely human terms she cannot do. It might be urged that in her final moments, Seneca accords Phaedra that capacity for moral action, equal to any man's, which Stoic doctrine insisted upon.[3]

Hippolytus is in turn now overshadowed by his stepmother. In Euripides' extant play his death is the great tragic moment of the drama, and his character is given a weight commensurate with its function. Seneca however has shifted the balance in favour of Phaedra, and his Hippolytus is accordingly less complex: something of his elemental quality is shown by his enthusiasm for the hunt, a matter that deserves a brief word. A surprising number of modern interpreters who are themselves squeamish about the pursuit of game regard hunting as indicative of Hippolytus' latent violence, and they claim that it is inconsistent with his ideal of the Golden Age. This interpretation relies upon a largely modern attitude to animals and their proper use by mankind. The robust Roman hunted for something to eat; of course he knew that killing was violent, but he did not kill game wantonly, even if he took pleasure in doing so. Even those most pacific of poets, Horace and Ovid, recommended hunting. Now to be sure Seneca in his youth had been persuaded by the Pythagorean philosopher, Sotion, to become a vegetarian for a while, but he nowhere condemns hunting as an activity. Well-to-do Romans enjoyed it, and Seneca's Hippolytus takes an unalloyed pleasure in the chase. When later on in his account of the Golden Age he speaks of laying snares to catch animals at lines 503-4, his point is that those were the only

4. Characterisation

snares men knew how to use in that blessed time: tricks were morally satisfactory if directed towards securing your dinner, they are obviously wrong when used against your fellow man. Hunting was generally regarded as manly, and moralists often contrasted it favourably with the life of luxury: that is Hippolytus' point in bringing hunting into his description of the Golden Age.[4]

Hippolytus' manner is in fact not usually violent: he shows polite concern for his family (lines 432-4). He exists of course to be the reluctant object of Phaedra's passion, and her frank focus, already noticed, upon his merely physical attractions renders unnecessary any profound psychological portrayal (she does not love him for his mind). Moreover, the absence of a divine element more or less ruled out a serious commitment to chastity as part of his make-up, as was argued above. Seneca's Hippolytus thus seems no more than uninterested in sex, a trait which the Nurse tries to overcome by urging him to 'lighten up' and enjoy his youth with its appropriate pleasures. As we have seen, his response to this advice is pretty generalised, and when it comes down to it, he is presented as little more than a stereotyped critic of womankind. A male Roman audience might have taken such a traditional posture in its stride, and not regarded it as unusual.

One aspect of his characterisation however does surprise and disturb. His reaction to Phaedra's direct assault upon his feelings is unexpected: he wants heaven to incinerate him with a lightening bolt (lines 682-3). This complicates his character somewhat, in that he realistically feels soiled by her attention, as if he had somehow encouraged it. His wish that he were dead seems an over-reaction, but there is a certain plausibility to it. This extreme response continues when Phaedra seeks his embrace (line 705); he does not merely repel her, or run away, like Joseph or Bellerophon:[5] he draws his sword to kill her. This is ugly, but again, realistic rather than heroic. The desire to harm does him no credit, but it is believable (and in terms of the plot his sword has to be secured somehow).

His final words on stage are again heartfelt. His sense of defilement is so strong, no amount of water can cleanse him (lines 715-18). His mind retreats for comfort into the charmed and (to him, at any rate) innocent world of the hunt: *o silvae, o ferae!* 'o woods, o beasts' (line 718). It is a moving moment. But that is not quite the last we see of him, for the Messenger describes his final moments and stresses his brave response to the appearance of bull from the sea at lines 1050-6: everywhere men and beasts – even hunter and hunted in the woods – had fled the apparition, only Hippolytus was unfazed (*solus immunis metu*, 1054). When the beast confronted his chariot, he dismissed it as an empty threat (*vanus ... terror*), the sort of thing his father, Theseus, was used to beating in a fight (see lines 1066-7, where Hippolytus has in mind both the Minotaur in Crete, and the Bull of Marathon, which Theseus had defeated in his youth). During the ensuing chase, he keeps his wits about him, and tries to manage his team. It is after all the horses which betray their master: Hippolytus is described as fearless throughout the ordeal.

The most recent reading of the characters of *Phaedra* is to be found in a stimulating essay by Hanna M. Roisman.[6] She regards Seneca's Phaedra as basically decent, with a genuine wish to be moral and good. But when Roisman speaks of her passion as 'irresistible' or claims that she would 'shun infidelity if she could', we may choose to part company with her interpretation. Such moral inevitability finds no place in Seneca's drama, since there is no divine instigator of Phaedra's love, nor does Roisman take due account of Phaedra's own admission that she is aware of the wrong she is doing (lines 594-9). Others find her wicked too (the Chorus at lines 824-8, for instance), but Roisman still misses in her the evil and resourcefulness she believed she disclosed in the Euripidean heroine (p. 77). She

4. Characterisation

fails however to consider the scene in which Seneca's Phaedra incriminates Hippolytus before Theseus. On his return from the Underworld, Theseus finds that his wife is determined to commit suicide, but she will not tell him why. This is resourcefulness on her part: she makes him make her talk, by his threat to torture the Nurse. But artfully, she does not talk plainly. Though she tells an outright lie at line 891 (she was of course not assailed by entreaties), when she describes the rape in line 892 as a violence done to her body, she merely equivocates, since as we 'the audience' saw, Hippolytus did indeed manhandle her, when he momentarily thought of killing her at lines 707-9. Theseus of course, as she intends, takes her expression to refer to something more terrible than Hippolytus' grabbing her by the hair. When he asks her who did it, she again does not lie outright, but says that the sword she kept to show him will 'tell' him who the rapist is (line 896). So without any direct lie, she manages to convince her husband that his son raped her. On balance, she is less of a victim and shows more in the way of evil resourcefulness than Roisman allows.

Roisman's account of Hippolytus is less controversial or original; she finds him brutal (a common enough view) and complex. The complexity she locates in the discrepancies and ambivalences of his praises of the Golden Age and life in the wilds. As has already been hinted, she is among those who take exception to his love of hunting, as if there were something obviously reprehensible about killing wild animals. Still, she rightly draws attention to a number of unexpected turns of phrase in his praises of country life which can be taken to subvert his message, and she concludes that Hippolytus seems less at peace in nature than he alleges (p. 81). When she concludes that nothing in his speech adequately explains why he chose the celibate life, many will agree with her. But the reason for the inadequacy may lie less in the characterisation of Hippolytus than in the failure of Seneca's own imagination to understand

Seneca: Phaedra

that there might be a positive attraction in virginity. He could only see it in negative terms, an avoidance of women based upon disgust at their sexual misdoings (lines 559-62).

The other, minor characters deserve a word. The Nurse has one dominant characteristic, her loyalty to Phaedra. She is used, as Seneca often uses a subordinate figure attached to a regal personage, to dissuade from wrong-doing. Also as usual, she fails. Loyalty turns her into an accomplice, so that she makes the initial approach to Hippolytus. When Phaedra's appeal has failed she unscrupulously plots the alleged rape, but it is left to Phaedra herself to incriminate Hippolytus before his father.[7]

Theseus' character is straightforward. Like an operatic hero, he must accept his wife's claims without investigation of their truth, and fall into a fit of imprudent rage. He regards his own son as a hypocrite (lines 915-22), and makes no effort to learn his side of the story, though Hippolytus' swift departure makes that impossible and even lends some credit to Phaedra's charge. But Theseus' portrayal is given an interesting twist by Seneca, in comparison to Euripides' father: he shows grief at the death of his son (lines 1114-17), attesting the strength of natural family ties (and thus reminding us of some of the leading themes of the play discussed above). In the last act, if staged, we again find ourselves confronted with something of a problem. When Phaedra appears sword in hand, Theseus make no effort to disarm her (he does not know yet that she is going to confess). Realistically considered, this would have been easy: as a woman she had no skill at swordplay, and he is a full-grown, fit man. He could easily wrest the sword from her, yet takes no action. It is odd. In the final scene grief and anger vie for control. He like Phaedra admits his own wrong-doing, and does all he can in purely human terms to make up for his curse: he cherishes the limbs of his dear son, and, in an unconscious echo of his wife, focuses upon the boy's physical beauty, now blasted (lines 1269-

4. *Characterisation*

70). He sets about preparing a funeral pyre on a regal scale. Phaedra he dismissively consigns to burial.

Tragic character

The analysis of the characterisation of individuals prompts reflection upon how Seneca might have regarded tragic character in general. The obvious question to ask is how his characters differ in this regard from those in his models (since it would be imprudent to suggest that the tragic quality of all characters in Greek drama can be defined in a straightforward way).

Euripides' Hippolytus is tragic partly because he is important enough to merit the direct attention of two divinities, one hostile. This at once establishes his heroic status. He is the companion of Artemis and the antagonist of Aphrodite. She for her part takes his antagonism seriously (as a god, she might dismiss it as trivial), and bends her efforts to destroying him. He is thus up against superior force, which there is no question of his defeating. The issue then becomes how he comports himself in the face of the inevitable. Here he shows another side to his character that, if not tragic, at least secures our sympathy: he is honourable against his own interest, in that he does not break the oath he gave the Nurse. Nothing similar makes Seneca's Hippolytus tragic, but he is not the focus of attention; it seems to be enough that he simply had bad luck.

Euripides' Phaedra is also tragic, though secondary in interest to Hippolytus, and for much the same reason: a god contrives her undoing, and she is up against an invincible force. But that force, Aphrodite, does her the credit of acknowledging her good name. Because Phaedra cannot live with her love for Hippolytus, and certainly has no strong intention of giving in to it, death seems her only option. What Seneca's Phaedra cannot live with is the absence of Hippolytus and perhaps too her guilty conscience, for having compassed the death of the innocent man she loved. But that is not tragic in the Greek sense. She grappled with her own feelings, not with a divinity, and moreover, those feelings were arguably (from the Nurse's point of view) not unmanageable. As the Nurse fairly says, it is those who are used to getting their own way, for example, royalty, who find it difficult to check their impulses, hardly grounds for tragedy if the situation goes 'pear-shaped'.

Seneca's tragic sensibility is therefore very unlike the Greek. But it would be a mistake to criticise him for this. Arguably he transformed the inherited material by modernising it. I have already referred more than once to the realism of the situations he depicts, and drawn attention to similar issues in the élite society of his time. By transfusing contemporary types of wrong-doing into a traditional mould he creates a new kind of tragic sensibility, in which the individual is alone with her own psyche, and has to come to terms with its defects. No external force is to blame, and attempts to inculpate fate or heredity are scouted. The philosopher and moralist in Seneca leaves the individual in charge of her own character, for better or worse. In short, the Senecan tragic character has a surprisingly modern look. Perhaps the most modern aspect of his characters, what most sets them apart from their Greek forebears, is their self-awareness. In Greek tragedy, ignorance is a powerful element in the tragic condition, but in Seneca the characters have a pretty clear idea of who they really are, and why they act as they do. Neither his Phaedra nor his Hippolytus lack self-knowledge (though Phaedra may try to shift the blame for her passion onto her heredity, she knows she has to live with its consequences). So there is not in Senecan tragedy that awakening to truth or reality that is so powerful in, say, Sophoclean drama (we might think of his Ajax, clutching his hair with his fists as he sits, a wreck amid the wreckage of slaughtered animals, or of Creon, aware at last of the power of his son's love for Antigone). For Seneca, the truth is always out in the open, and his characters

4. Characterisation

know it; the tragic issue is a modern one: coming to terms with a reality we always knew was there. We are much more sympathetic to this sort of tragic situation, since most of our tragic writers since the Renaissance, especially those of the Nordic dramatists of the late nineteenth century, have followed lines very similar to his. There is no divine, external force operating upon Hedda Gabler, she is alone with her own damaged soul. Seneca's *Phaedra*, whilst not perhaps as refined an investigation of psychic damage, is nonetheless of that tradition, indeed arguably he initiated it.

Two other factors contribute to the unusual nature of Seneca's tragic characters, namely the mythical tradition, especially as inherited from drama, and the rhetorical mode of argument on which the plays are so often built. Let us consider the role of the mythical tradition first.

When Seneca decided to write on any tragic theme, the main lines of the story were not something he felt he could depart from. Thus, in our play, Phaedra must love Hippolytus, and he must reject her at the cost of his life; Theseus must be the agent of his destruction through his curse. There is a sort of mythological determinism at work here. The early Greek playwrights had had considerable freedom to invent important details; Euripides for instance is reckoned to have introduced the notion that Medea deliberately killed her children into his drama on that theme. But that innovation became fixed in the tradition, and Medea ever after must kill her children to spite Jason. Thus Seneca finds himself with a good number of fixed points for his dramas, and these fixed points largely determined his approach to character and motivation as well. Thus in the case of Hippolytus, for instance, he did not like Racine invent a girlfriend for him to account for his lack of interest in Phaedra. His character remained that of a misogynist, whatever the reason. Seneca felt that he needed no more than that to generate the tragic situation. We see something similar in his treatment of

Seneca: Phaedra

Theseus. By Roman standards, Theseus' action in cursing his son to death was outrageous; a Roman father would have needed to seek the advice of a family council, and anyway no prudent man would act so drastically on hearing an unsupported charge of rape. But Theseus has to curse his son, that is an inherited part of the story. So Seneca has him do it in a fit of rage, however unsatisfactory that may be in human terms. (Even in dramatic terms it is somewhat unsatisfactory, since both Euripides and Racine engineered a confrontation between son and father, so that Hippolytus has at least a theoretical chance to exculpate himself.) Thus character in its broad outlines is predetermined for Seneca by the mythical tradition, and he is at no great pains to deepen or nuance it.

Rhetoric also has a role to play in his approach to characterisation. Drama sets up situations in which people have to justify their actions to themselves or to each other. The situations tend to be adversarial, and the characters, whose actions as we have seen are pretty much predetermined, have simply to set out their case. When for instance in our play the Nurse has urged Hippolytus to adopt a less austere life style, he has only to stick to his guns for the tragedy to unfold along traditional lines. So all Seneca needed was a speech setting out the grounds for an aversion from women. They do not have to be especially cogent or persuasive, nor do they have to be at all personal; they suffice if they help Hippolytus in sustaining his obstinacy. They do not have to satisfy anyone else, including the critical reader. Similarly Phaedra's change of heart in the early part of the play is rhetorically generated. She starts out as a victim of her erotic passion (*furor*), and the Nurse tries to argue her out of it. She is too successful, and all of a sudden at line 250 Phaedra agrees to her point that such a love is disgraceful, and so she determines to die, without considering alternative measures (in Racine, Phèdre had sent Hippolytus away from Athens to Troezen). The Nurse is horrified, immediately climbs down from her former

4. Characterisation

moral high ground, and undertakes to bend Hippolytus to his stepmother's desires. Once again what we are presented with is a rhetorical (i.e. adversarial) presentation of a predetermined situation. Phaedra must love Hippolytus, and she may, for decency's sake, try to fight it; but in the end, someone – Phaedra herself, the Nurse, or both together – must present the erotic opportunity to the intransigent young man. Seneca puts arguments into the mouths of his characters that will get the action to the required point; to put this another way, motivation is purely local. He is not concerned to design characters with hidden depths or rounded personalities (this consideration should be borne in mind by those like Roisman and Segal who analyse his text with such subtlety). He provides just enough ground for the Nurse's change of heart and for Hippolytus' misogyny to keep the story on the traditional rails. More was not wanted, since the plot required simply that the Nurse be an agent in the intrigue and that the young man have an invincible loathing of womankind. Their 'personal' reasons in either case were immaterial.

5

Literary Texture

I noted earlier, in my account of the development of tragedy at Rome, that most of the early playwrights built on Greek foundations. This was in fact the procedure of all the great literary artists of Rome: Catullus and Virgil, Cicero and Sallust all at one time or another took Greek authors as their models for imitation. Now imitation has been repudiated occasionally in the later western literary tradition, but for the ancient Roman it was the obvious way to succeed: what had pleased longest, pleased most, and the successful Greeks could show the way to best literary practice. But imitation was never the whole story. The Roman wanted to do better than his model, and one of the devices employed was the blending of sources. We encounter this as early as the comic poets Plautus and Terence, who combined different parts of several plays (in fact the practice, nowadays called *contaminatio*, was frowned upon by some writers, but defended by Terence). The point was to achieve by synthesis as powerful a drama as possible by excerpting the best elements from the best models. Perhaps the classic example of this blending of sources is found in Virgil's *Aeneid*, which is built up out of episodes from not only two Homeric epics, the *Iliad* and the *Odyssey*, but also from the *Argonautica* of Apollonius of Rhodes. Virgil thus blended elements from a number of sources into a new synthesis of the epic tradition. His own practice had been developed for over a century before him and remained dominant in the production of Latin literature down to the time of Seneca and beyond. So when Seneca began to write tragedy it was quite natural for him both to build upon a Greek foundation, and to blend his sources.

Another point needs to be made that has a bearing upon drama in particular. We think of plays as entertainments to be performed on a stage. So of course did the Greeks and Romans, but the later playwrights themselves regarded drama as a literary tradition: scripts had become texts (this is very evident from the sort of rules and regulations for the composition of drama that we find in Horace's *Art of Poetry*). In fact, Athenian drama, particularly Euripides, was, alongside Homer, the cornerstone of education in the Greek world, and the texts of the plays were studied avidly because poetic literature was felt to embody what was best in Hellenic culture (despite Plato's protests). So the great plays were known chiefly through reading, and that makes a considerable difference to their reception, especially their reception by later playwrights. In short, the tradition is no longer purely dramatic, but has a purely literary element to it as well.

Many playwrights in Athens choose the same myth for their dramas; Philoctetes, for instance, was the subject of tragedies by Aeschylus, Sophocles, and Euripides. It was unusual for an author to return to the same myth more than once, but that was the case with Euripides, who, as we have seen, twice represented the love of Phaedra for Hippolytus on stage. It was possible for Seneca therefore to blend Greek dramatic models, just as Virgil was to blend his epic ones, and we find him exploiting this opportunity in his reworking of the Phaedra myth. It is important to bear in mind as well that by Seneca's day tragic form and diction were well integrated into the Roman literary tradition, and we should not expect from him any close adherence to one, or more, Greek originals.[1] Those scripts will in some cases have had Latin adaptations, or have been worked into non-tragic forms, such as epic or elegy, all of which Seneca will have been acquainted with. It is for instance clear that he

5. *Literary Texture*

exploited Ovid's *Heroides* 4, a letter from Phaedra to Hippolytus. At the outset, however, Phaedra ought to have evoked for him, and for his audience, the notorious Hippolytus-dramas of Euripides (Sophocles too wrote a *Phaedra*, now lost but for fragments). We must then be slow to disengage Seneca from his models (Roman as well as Greek), because the myths came to him embodied in a literary tradition of texts.

Seneca had, unusually, two plays of Euripides on which to draw for his re-enactment of the love of Phaedra for Hippolytus.[2] Tradition related that Euripides' first version was unsuccessful, because Phaedra and the Nurse were depicted as shameless (details are not given: did Phaedra for instance do little to resist her passion, and induce the Nurse to approach Hippolytus?);[3] this version is now lost but for fragments. The second version, performed in 428 BC, was very successful, and this time the character of Phaedra was markedly different. For our purposes what is important is that Seneca clearly blended elements from both plays, and the characterisation of Phaedra in particular owes much to this process of attempted integration. We see something of his method in the opening scene.[4] In the extant play by Euripides Hippolytus returns from the hunt, and offers thanks to Artemis. Seneca reverses the action: Hippolytus is setting off for the hunt, and prays to Diana (= Artemis) for success. Or consider the absence of Theseus, necessary for Phaedra's decision to get to grips with Hippolytus. We do not know why he was absent in Euripides' first version; in the second, extant version he is away on a visit to an oracle (which suggests that he will be back soon). Seneca accounts for his absence differently: Theseus has accompanied his friend Pirithous on a journey to the Underworld to ravish Persephone. This changes the mood altogether: Theseus may never return, Phaedra feels cheated and alone (lines 91-2). But the source of that motif is almost certainly, for Seneca, Ovid *Heroides* 4.109-12 (though Ovid may have derived it from one of the now lost versions by Euripides or Sophocles). This is the sort of blending of literary sources that Roman writers cultivated. Of course, blending is not enough in itself; the mixture must be harmonious, and here Seneca has arguably failed in the attempt to integrate his sources into a new whole, as we can demonstrate.

Let a simple example start the analysis. In the first act the Nurse, to prevent Phaedra from committing suicide, undertakes to tackle Hippolytus herself (this strategy comes from Euripides' second version). But at lines 427-8 she remarks how difficult it is to venture on a 'delegated crime' (*mandatum scelus*). Has she forgotten herself so soon? More likely, Seneca has inopportunely recalled the first version of the Euripidean play, in which, as I have suggested, the erotic initiative may have been shameless Phaedra's. If *Phaedra* was one of Seneca's first attempts at tragic composition, such irregularities may be ascribed to his inexperience.

Rather more glaring for some critics is the unsettled characterisation of Phaedra. She appears in the first act resolute and in control, albeit emotionally dismayed, but the motivation for her sudden decision to die at lines 250-4 is worse than sketchy. In the second act she is confused and ill. How has this come about? Coffey would rather not see this as a cumbersome mingling of different sources,[5] but that is the likeliest explanation for the incoherent presentation of the aspects of Phaedra's character (that, and the possible inexperience of the author, new to this genre). There were two Euripidean Phaedras: one shameless, and possibly resolute, the other indecisive and revolted by her own feelings for her stepson. Seneca wanted both in his play. There is nothing intrinsically wrong with that, but we have a right to test the success of the synthesis. Some regard it as a failed experiment: the integration never takes place. Others, like Coffey, argue for a delineation of moral decline, of which the physical and mental exhaustion are symbolic. But there is arguably even more to it than that, and once again the

5. Literary Texture

issue is the literary texture of the play. Seneca was not just indebted to previous drama, but to all of previous poetry, particularly the great Augustan poets of an earlier generation. His depiction of Phaedra, for instance, owes a considerable debt to Virgil's Dido, as described by Elaine Fantham.[6] The characterisation of Phaedra therefore is complex, and owes a great deal to the long Graeco-Roman literary tradition. But that was how Roman writers approached their business, through literature.

Seneca continues to mix his versions in the play (we assume). He departs from the second Euripidean play by dispensing with a meeting between Hippolytus and Theseus before the curse, and in having Phaedra admit her part in her stepson's downfall before committing suicide. We might ascribe both of these decisions to his use of the first Euripidean version, or to deployment of Sophocles' *Phaidra*, or even to an impulse of originality. He reserved his most remarkable borrowing for the last scene, by adapting the ending of Euripides' *Bacchae* to conclude his own play.[7] Unfortunately the *Bacchae* is defective just at this point, but it is clear from the play's hypothesis that Cadmus collected up the limbs of his daughter's son Pentheus (she and her sisters had torn him apart on Mount Cithaeron during a Bacchic orgy). Again, Seneca abandons the second version by Euripides, in which the dying Hippolytus is brought on stage to be reconciled to his father, and instead has him killed outright in the destruction of his chariot. His body is then shattered as the horses run amok, and the pieces are retrieved by his servants, who bring them onstage to Theseus, similarly to what happened at the end of the *Bacchae*. An élite Roman audience will have expected that sort of recombination of elements drawn from the dramatic tradition. (Of course they may also have felt that it was tastelessly managed in this case.)

Phaedra is a drama, but it is also, and perhaps in Seneca's case primarily, a poetic text. Just as the dramatic action is owed to a remix of Greek tragedies, so the verbal texture is heavily indebted to recycling phraseology from the works of the Augustan giants, Virgil, Horace (particularly in the choral lyrics of the play), and above all Ovid. Once again, this was a feature that would have appealed to the original élite audience, and Seneca's exploitation of his Latin models is as much a part of his method as is his debt to the Greeks. The Nurse provides a straightforward example of such borrowing: she has clearly 'read' her Ovid.[8] Ovid, after composing a three-book didactic poem on how to make love, wrote a clever palinode in one book, *Remedia Amoris* ('Antidotes against Love'), in which he pointed out that easy-living provides the seed bed for lust (lines 743-4). The Nurse, when she denounces extravagance at line 204 onwards, is plainly acquainted with his doctrine and takes an equally robust line.

Hippolytus too has 'read' Ovid, as his response to the proposition of the Nurse makes plain. He argues that his life in the woods keeps him close to the ideals of the Golden Age.[9] His description of primitive times in lines 527-39 is an adroit blend of two passages from Ovid, *Amores* 3.8.41-8 and *Metamorphoses* 1.94-102, which even preserves precisely the order in which the topics were handled by Ovid: first, there were no boundary stones on land; secondly, no one sailed the sea, which was taken to be a natural barrier not to be transgressed; thirdly, men had no defences or weapons, and finally agriculture was unknown in primitive times. The first point is only in the *Amores*, the last only in the *Metamorphoses*, but all are in Hippolytus' speech!

Seneca is not, however, just an imitator, but he is capable of launching out into original literary conceits, generally after the fashion of Ovid. It is remarkable too how often in the choral odes of his plays Seneca shows an Ovidian love of witty paradox or humour. To take but one instance from our play, the Chorus sing at lines 309-16 of how the Moon-goddess, Diana, when she went courting, handed over her chariot to her big brother, the Sun-

5. Literary Texture

god, Apollo, to drive. But the 'car' was built for her, not him, and his size slowed down the course of the moon through the night sky. This is amusing and Ovid would have been proud of his pupil, just as Seneca's audience would have appreciated the mythological travesty in the best Ovidian tradition. There may too be an implicit comparison between the light-hearted dalliance of the gods and the misery of mortals in love.[10]

Another aspect of the literary tone of the play to which attention has incidentally been drawn from time to time is its indebtedness to rhetoric. Seneca himself was trained in the rhetorical tradition by a father devoted to the declamatory performances of the Augustan age. In his youth he made his name in the law courts, and all of his writings display the *nitor* (stylistic 'glossiness') fashionable at the time. An extended example of the rhetorical tradition at work in *Phaedra* has also already been noted, but can now be discussed more fully. The appeal of the Nurse (lines 435-82) and Hippolytus' reply (lines 483-564) perhaps strike the modern reader as strange, since there is little in the way of a personal note in either. They do not seem to engage with one another as individuals in a particular situation. The reason for this may be sought in the rhetorical tradition in which Seneca and his audience were educated. Rhetoric taught you how to make a case convincing; it did not necessarily deal in *ad hominem* arguments, but sought a high, generalised ground. The Nurse operates on that assumption in producing what is in effect a speech of generalised persuasion, what the Romans called a *suasoria*, related to a common debating theme: 'Should a man marry?' The inference to be drawn from such generalised arguments is that what is good for someone is good for everyone. The Nurse deploys two common-sense arguments, first, that youth is the time for pleasure (lines 443-65), and secondly, that the world needs repopulating (lines 466-82); each case is strengthened by divine sanction for the use of right time and of sex (lines 451 and 466). She can thus

Seneca: Phaedra

conclude in words that must remind us of the author's own Stoicism, that Hippolytus should take Nature as his guide in life (line 481). Hippolytus' reply is, as I have argued above, equally rhetorical, in that he gives a purely generalised account (which, as we have just seen, owes much to Ovid) of the decline of human morality over time. A moralist might pin the cause of decline on any number of factors; Hippolytus does here become more 'case specific' in that he chooses women, but still, given the misogynistic strain in much ancient thought, this is not highly individualised. (We might here compare the sixth satire of Juvenal, another rhetorically generated attack upon marriage, which always draws attention to the immorality of wives.) Hippolytus' rejection of women is to be seen in this context. Despite his possessing a specific character in the play, he is not bothered to account for his disposition (see line 567); Seneca seems simply to assume that his attitude would have been understandable to the audience within the long tradition of literary and rhetorical misogyny. The whole of the exchange may not prove to our minds very dramatic, but to the contemporary Roman audience, with its greater taste for rhetorically developed argument, the deployment of two opposed points of view had its own appeal.

I have referred to the *nitor* or 'glossiness' of contemporary style. The hallmarks of this in Seneca's day were brevity of expression and the use of epigram (called *sententia* in Latin). (Both features make conveying the tone of his plays in translation very difficult.) He achieved brevity chiefly in two ways, either by leaving out ideas that the audience must supply for itself, or through learned allusion to characters or situations in myth. An example of a compressed thought occurs in line 174. The Nurse has been warning Phaedra against the incest she proposes to commit with Hippolytus, and reminds her of the awful fruit of her mother's liaison with the bull, namely the Minotaur (now dead). She asks why do monsters cease, why is

5. Literary Texture

her brother's stall empty? This is an ironical and elliptical challenge to Phaedra to produce an abominable offspring of her own from an illicit affair, and hide it away in a labyrinth. Similar is line 1153 where the Chorus say that the reckoning is balanced for the infernal king, meaning that though Pluto, king of the Underworld, has lost Theseus (who escaped after the attempted rape of Proserpine), he has gained Hippolytus. (This may well strike us as a rather frigid conceit which detracts from the tragic situation.) A comparative adjective lends itself to ellipse, for instance at line 1239, where Theseus proposes to follow his son in death to the Underworld and assures Chaos that his present journey is 'more fitting' (*iustior*). He means 'more fitting' than his previous journey, when with Pirithous he sought to ravish the Queen of Hades. Such elliptical expressions of thought seem better designed to appeal to readers than to a live audience, which is unlikely to catch them or have time to decode them.

Allusions are extremely common, especially the identification of a god or mythological character by an epithet or roundabout form of expression. One of the trickiest allusions in *Phaedra* is found at line 245, where the Nurse is trying to convince her mistress to abandon any thought of seducing Hippolytus. She mentions the people who will stand in Phaedra's way or punish her wrongdoing. After mentioning her husband, Theseus, the Nurse says, 'Your father will be here', a reference to Minos, King of Crete. Phaedra replies, riddlingly, 'Do you mean Ariadne's gentle father?' This is hard to understand: Ariadne was Phaedra's sister, and had also loved Theseus, to the extent of helping him kill her half-brother, the Minotaur, and running away with him. What Phaedra seems to be hinting at with the word 'gentle' (*mitis*) is that Minos, so the traditional story went, had made no effort to pursue that absconded couple, which makes her feel that he is unlikely to bother himself about her own sexual misconduct. It is a very

Seneca: Phaedra

teasing allusion to a little-remarked aspect of the myth. Again, it is the sort of allusive learnedness a reader rather than a live audience is likely to latch onto, and we here too detect something of the strongly textual character of the play.

Epigrams are common throughout the play (see, for example, lines 139, 140-1, 215, 249, 430, 607, 735, 878), but they are not a trivial stylistic game, despite the obvious use of word play in their formulation. Seneca makes it clear in his prose works that poetry often has a power beyond prose to encapsulate a moral truth so that it will remain memorable. His own frequent quotations from poetry illustrate that he believed what he said, and the moral epigrams thickly sown through his own plays are designed to crystallise the sort of instruction which Seneca felt poetry could offer its readers. His prose works too are filled with memorable moral epigrams, and they are one of the common features of his writing.

6

Reception and Later Influence

How were Seneca's tragedies received in his own lifetime? In all of his still abundant writing he never referred to himself as a playwright or poet; he may have subscribed to the traditional Roman view that poetry was less suitable than prose as an instrument for serious discourse. Certainly his own pronouncements on poetry suggest that Seneca tended to this view, and believed that the chief aim of poetry was entertainment. That said, the entertainment should not be morally neutral, and Seneca allowed that poetry often had a force that prose lacked, as we have just seen. Still, the lack of reference in his extant works to his own efforts as a poet-playwright suggests that he may have set less store by his scripts than by his many philosophical writings in prose. It is even possible that he did not himself publish his tragedies, but that they were made available only after his death by his devoted followers. We may nonetheless assume that they enjoyed some measure of contemporary success in performance (a point to be discussed below) since he wrote at least seven complete tragedies, and left one uncompleted (*Phoenician Women*). A busy and intelligent man presumably would not have thrown away his time and effort on a failed enterprise.

The success of the dramas was however ephemeral. We can say this with some assurance, owing to the absence of any reference to them in the so-called canon of classical authors and

Seneca: Phaedra

texts compiled on the basis of popular opinion in the tenth book of the *Institutio oratoria* by Quintilian in the 90s AD (Quintilian in fact gives it as his opinion that the best tragic poet of his day was Pomponius Secundus.) This is not to say however that the plays were entirely neglected: Quintilian himself quotes a line from the *Medea* (453 is cited at *Institutio oratoria* 9.2.8), and later poets, Statius for instance, are clearly acquainted with the texts. But the exclusion of them from the body of the 'canon', which cannot be a whim of Quintilian's, suggests that they had not achieved the sort of acknowledged classic status that would encourage later writers to imitate them. By the same token we might assume that they were no longer performed, in any medium.

But they continued to be read and exploited by some authors. The fourth-century poet Prudentius turned to *Phaedra* for the composition of one of his 'Christian ballads', celebrating the feast-day (13 August) of the martyrdom of the Roman presbyter, Hippolytus.[1] Hymn 11 of the *Peristephanon* ('Crowns of Martyrdom') describes a painting of the martyrdom of the saint, seen by Prudentius, which depicted him being torn limb from limb by wild horses. (Hippolytus up until the moment of his death had been a schismatic, i.e. he taught doctrines not approved by the Church and so 'tore' the unity of the faith; the form of his death was therefore peculiarly appropriate.) The painting is reckoned to have existed, but its inspiration may have been the Greek legend rather than oral tradition or historical fact. More important for our purpose is the exploitation of the Messenger speech in *Phaedra* for details of the act of martyrdom. The old man is bound to a pair of untamed horses, which are lashed to a fury and set free to run. Their career begins at line 111 and ends at line 122, much of the detail being taken from our play. Then Prudentius describes another scene in the painting, sorrowful followers who come to recover the shattered limbs, rather as the servants bring in the bits and pieces left of Hippolytus; there is

6. Reception and Later Influence

one difference: the Christians recover *all* the limbs of their martyr. Prudentius even manages to outdo Seneca by having them collect with sponges the martyr's blood from sand, rock, and thorn-bushes!

Prudentius' use of a painting suggests that we might look for other images in classical antiquity which arguably owe a similar debt to Seneca. Here we are necessarily on less certain ground: Pascale Linant de Bellefonds is duly cautious in tracing the origins of the representations in mosaic and relief of Hippolytus and Phaedra without the Nurse. We note, for instance, that generally in such depictions Hippolytus holds a letter (the means by which Phaedra revealed her feelings), so Senecan influence is clearly ruled out. De Bellefonds describes what may be a scene of Hippolytus threatening to kill Phaedra on a wall painting from Pompeii, now in Naples; it is of the time of Vespasian, i.e. not long after Seneca's death (but other interpretations are possible). Similarly uncertain is the suggested representation of the suicide of Phaedra over the corpse of Hippolytus.[2]

The last important author in antiquity who made clear use of our play is Boethius. As a courtier and philosopher, who fell into disgrace under a tyrant, he may well have felt some sympathy with Seneca. Whatever the motive, in his *Consolation of Philosophy* the fifth lyric of the first book is heavily indebted to the third choral song of the play (beginning at line 959) in which the indifference of god and nature is emphasised by the domination of chance (*fortuna*) in human affairs.[3] It should be said that writers like Prudentius and Boethius turn to Seneca less as a dramatist than as an admired author, whose writings provided the stimulus of traditional thoughts and model expressions.

Thereafter Senecan drama suffered the general eclipse of so much else in Latin literature, though parts of his tragedies continued to be known in some form or other. In a brief, authori-

Seneca: Phaedra

tative account of the circulation of his text, R.J. Tarrant observes that it was in the fourteenth century that the popularity of the tragedies began to grow rapidly.[4] Then for the first time a commentary was produced upon the play, by the English Dominican Nicholas Trevet, to enable readers to decode the references to myth and geography; something more will be said about this commentary in Chapter 7 below.

The scene between Phaedra and the Nurse and the first choral song on the power of love were appropriated by Aeneas Silvius Piccolomini (later Pope Pius II) for the opening of his novella *De Duobus Amantibus* ('The Two Lovers'), written in the early 1440s. A noble and married Sienese lady, Lucretia, falls in love with a German knight, Euryalus. She tries to get her husband's servant Sosia to help her in her erotic predicament. He counsels chastity and prudence, she says she cannot live with her love and threatens suicide, he knuckles under: all of this, including much of the actual script, is taken from our play (Piccolomini wrote in Latin, though the work was soon much disseminated in translation as well). The borrowings are conveniently noted in the footnotes to an edition of the novella with modern German translation by Herbert Rädle, *Euryalus und Lucretia* (Stuttgart: Reclam, 1993).

From the Renaissance onwards Seneca's plays served as models for the composition of tragedies either in Latin (a once-flourishing industry among humanists) or in the vernacular. Since Greek was altogether less accessible to many writers it is not surprising that their attraction to the tale of Phaedra will have been owed to Seneca rather than Euripides. Furthermore Senecan drama had the merit of simple (if at times incoherent) structure, and an action less integrated into a specific religious mentality than the Greek. French tragedians in particular adapted Seneca's version to the vernacular.[5] The most famous of these is by Robert Garnier (1544/5-1590), whose *Hippolyte* was published in 1573.[6] Certain characters' roles have been

6. Reception and Later Influence

fleshed out, chiefly that of the Nurse (who expresses remorse for her entrapment of Hippolytus, and commits suicide), and also there are some refinements in characterisation: Hippolytus is no brute and does not draw his sword on Phaedra, while she is depicted as more reserved. The overall tone is domestic and intimate. Garnier changed too the moral liability of the characters: heredity is no longer seen as a cause of crime. This alteration was presumably generated by a Christian's sense of absolute moral responsibility. Still, it is significant that Garnier did not shirk the incestuous character of Phaedra's attraction to Hippolytus; some adapters (for example, Bidar) removed this by having her still only engaged to Theseus, and not yet his wife.

Whether *Hippolyte* was ever performed or not is uncertain, but Garnier's instinct that some Senecan stage action could not be successfully represented has already been mentioned above, where his omission of Phaedra's awkward aside was noted (p. 25). He showed himself equally alert to the problem of the Chorus' denunciation of Phaedra's possible dumbshow at 824-8 (also discussed above, pp. 52-3): he omitted it! Finally, and once again anticipating his successor Claus, he has Hippolytus' body brought on intact at the end. The Senecan 'reconstruction' of the young man's corpse proved too much for his sense of decorum. Thus three of the most problematic pieces of action in the Senecan original are quietly put right by Garnier, who sensed what could plausibly be managed on the stage.

Brief mention should also be made of a subsequent adaptation of Seneca, La Pinelière's *Hippolyte*, performed in 1635.[7] Though it is not now highly regarded, it is significant for ensuring that it was a Senecan Phaedra who dominated the French stage. It has been noted that La Pinelière is even more faithful to the Senecan action than Garnier, and that he went further in adapting the characterisation to French taste. He thus formed a bridge for the greatest dramatic artist to revisit the Senecan site, Jean Racine (1639-99).

Seneca: Phaedra

Racine obviously needed to put some distance between himself and his predecessors, but he was happy to borrow from the Roman playwright in spite of his professed debt to Euripides. His *Phèdre* of 1677 is generally regarded as his masterpiece, and it was his last tragedy on a classical theme, the culmination of his career. In composing his plot he had had an advantage over his predecessors, in that he had learned Greek in the Jansenist school at Port-Royal (Paris),[8] and so could read Euripides in the original (to be sure, if his predecessors had been keen they could have read Euripides in dual-language texts, Greek and Latin). With the intellectual snobbery that so often complements a knowledge of Greek he never allowed in his *Préface* to *Phèdre* that he nonetheless owed a considerable debt to Seneca (who is however named). Ronald W. Tobin has claimed that 'as a matter of fact, Racine follows Seneca's lead in almost every instance where Seneca deviates from the Euripidean version'.[9] This is seen above all in the shift of interest from Hippolytus to Phaedra herself. Racine has also taken over Phaedra's avowal of love,[10] the use of Hippolytus' own sword as evidence against him, and Phaedra's exoneration of the young man and suicide on stage (actually she has taken poison before she appears for the last time). Likewise in Racine it is the nurse, Oenone, who comes up with the plot against Hippolyte, and Thésée is allowed to show a natural grief at having contrived his son's death (in Euripides the father is impassive). Finally, Racine follows Seneca rather than Euripides in not bringing the son and father together at the very end so that they can be reconciled to one another; Hippolyte dies off stage. It is however above all for the character of Phèdre that Racine is most indebted to Seneca.

Phèdre's sexual arousal, her sense of responsibility for what has happened, and her attempted seduction of her beloved are all drawn from the Roman dramatist. As Tobin puts it: 'the daring, sensual side of Seneca's creations was understood by

6. Reception and Later Influence

Racine as it never had been by his predecessors' (p. 146). We see this understanding and exploitation of a model in tiny details of borrowing; for example, Seneca's Phaedra had said at lines 646-7 that she loved in Hippolytus the features she recognised as having been those of his young father, when she first saw him in Crete. Racine's Phèdre at first reverses the idea, and says that she cannot look at her husband without seeing Hippolyte (line 290: 'Mes yeux le retrouvaient dans les traits de son père'). Later, when confronted with Hippolyte (and believing Thésée dead), she redeploys the Senecan model more fully, and says that Thésée is not dead, so long as she sees him in his son, as he himself was as a young man (lines 627-8); then at lines 638-52 Racine re-elaborates the Senecan description of his looks and even picks up the conceit of lines 661-2 that if Hippolyte had gone to Crete with Thésée, it would have been for him instead that Ariadne unwound the thread into the Labyrinth. The representation of a woman's sexual frustration was a significant innovation on the French stage, and Racine was clearly inspired by admiration for Seneca's passionate, unrestrained 'heroine', endowed with a tremendous, if destructive, energy.

Tobin also notices the point discussed above, that Racine exploits the theme of misfortune within the family (p. 149), an issue absent from the heroic tragedies of his senior contemporary, Corneille. The final point to which he draws attention (p. 150), again noticed above, is the general sense of hopelessness in Senecan tragedy. Whereas Euripides' play ended with human reconciliation and the promise of divine revenge, Seneca leaves us with a void, the ruin of a family. Theseus is desolated: his wife betrayed him and his son is dead by his own wish (the other children are conveniently forgotten at this point). This conclusion to the action possibly appealed to a pessimistic streak in Racine that his Jansenism nourished, and he was drawn to it rather than to the Euripidean ending, in which a god directly effects reconciliation between the human beings. What some of

Seneca: Phaedra

Racine's modern students have overlooked, however, is that he realised this bleakness by adopting yet again a Senecan strategy, the complete omission of the gods from the action. The characters may, as in Seneca, invoke the gods, or blame them for what is happening, or attribute sin to the force of heredity, but without the actual presence of the gods we may construe all this as the despairing attempts of mortals to come to terms with what they cannot explain or account for in rational terms. Why have their lives come to grief in this way? Their answers are many, sometimes inconsistent, but never more than provisional. Seneca has virtually marginalised the gods, and a similar concept of God's infinite remoteness (the hidden God, 'Le Dieu caché') was central to Jansenist mentality. Racine thus responded to Seneca both as a dramatic artist and as a religious sensibility.

Of course Racine made changes too, most notably in the provision of a lover for Hippolyte, the maiden Aricie. It has been suggested that this was necessary at the time, since a considerable number of the royal court would have assumed that an Hippolytus uninterested in women must be, like themselves, homosexual.[11] Be that as it may, the character of Hippolyte is certainly gentler. Phèdre too is characterised in a more moral light, in that her attraction to Hippolyte is only unleashed when she receives word (false, in the event) that Thésée is dead. Still, once she has set about her avowal, she knows no restraint; this scene is fully analysed by John Lapp.[12] Racine, as just noted, conceives of Hippolyte rather differently from Seneca; in a word he gallicises him, and makes him more of a gentleman (though there are certainly glimpses of this quality in Seneca). Thus during the great scene of avowal – 'perhaps the most powerful in Racinian tragedy' according to Lapp (p. 173) – Hippolyte is stunned into paralysis. He is too immobilised to react, and certainly unable to draw his sword. Phèdre therefore has to do it herself, and this scene, entirely absent from the older Garnier

6. Reception and Later Influence

adaptation, brought down upon Racine's head considerable criticism: it was too lively for the French stage of the day! But so famous did the action become that it was repeatedly chosen for illustration, for example, by Hubert Gravelot, as the frontispiece for the play in an eighteenth-century edition.[13] And yet the character of Phèdre is, like that of Hippolyte, softened to accord more with the French sense of decorum: she does not accuse him of rape herself, that is left to Oenone (and indeed the accusation is made off-stage).[14]

One other portion of Racine's play is heavily indebted to Seneca, namely the report of the death of Hippolyte, here given by his companion, Théramène. This renowned 'récit [speech] de Théramène' (Act 5, Scene 6, 1498-1592) surprisingly owes a more considerable debt to Seneca than to Euripides.[15] For example, Racine follows Seneca in having the first dreadful noise come from the sea; Hippolyte's reaction to the appearance of the sea monster – he throws a spear at it – is a development of lines 1066-7 of Seneca's version, in which Hippolytus declares that he is not afraid of the beast; and to Seneca are owed the grisly details of the bloodstained track leading to the body, and the bushes strewn with Hippolyte's hair. On the other hand, Racine rightly felt that the numerous similes used by Seneca's Messenger clogged the narrative, and smacked too much of epic narrative, rather than dramatic, so he dispensed with them. By the same token, he reduced the length of the description of the bull from the sea; in Seneca it extends over fourteen lines (1035-49), in Racine it takes up no more than five (1517-21). (Euripides, however, had made do with two words, 'wild monster' [1214]!)[16]

Senecan drama was rather under a cloud through the eighteenth and nineteenth centuries, but a remarkable echo of his sensibility was developed in a tragic *scena* by A.C. Swinburne, 'Phaedra', published in the first collection of *Poems and Ballads* (London: Moxon, 1866).[17] The scene depicts Phaedra encouraging Hippolytus to kill her with his sword. Now plainly Euripides is not the source of the action (despite the presence of a Chorus of Troezenian women, a false lead). Only in Seneca and Racine did Phaedra confront Hippolytus directly (and Swinburne was well acquainted with both classical and French literature), and only in them does the women embrace the prospect of death at the hands of the man she loves. It was that which appealed to the deliquescent eroticism of Swinburne, who spins out Phaedra's plea for some pages. The springboard is line 704 of our play, where Hippolytus tells Phaedra not to touch him. Swinburne's heroine insists that he draw his sword to kill her (Racine's revision of Seneca). He refuses and flees, leaving Phaedra to her own thoughts. She is depicted in Senecan colours. She dwells for instance on his physicality ('godlike for great brows / Thou art, and thewed as gods are, with clear hair', reminiscent of lines 651-6). More Senecan yet is the final monologue in which Phaedra traces her own passion back to her mother, Pasiphae ('she hath sown pain and plague in all our house ... marriage-fodder snuffed about of kine'). That isolated scene in its turn had a considerable influence upon Gabriele D'Annunzio, who produced a *Fedra* in 1909, which owes very little to the earlier dramatic tradition, though he claimed rightly that his heroine was closer to Seneca's than to any other's.[18] The point to re-emphasise is that Seneca was the first to be frank about Phaedra's erotic yearning, and later artists of quite different sensibility were able to follow his lead and develop that characteristic in their own ways.

Two contemporary dramatists, Hugo Claus (1929-) and Sarah Kane (1971-99), have engaged closely with our tragedy. The Fleming Claus, reckoned the leading contemporary Dutch-language playwright, wrote *Phaedra (naar Seneca)* in 1980.[19] A considerable portion of his output is devoted to the adaptation of classical themes and scripts, and *Phaedra* is the third of his engagements with Seneca (it should be mentioned that the

6. Reception and Later Influence

classic Dutch poet, Joost van den Vondel [1587-1679] produced a dramatic version of this myth in 1628). Claus has said that what especially attracts him to Seneca is that he is not a classically perfect writer (such command admiration, but not emulation); he is himself drawn to Seneca's mannerism, sensationalism, and the general discordance of his composition.[20] Claus' own version was recently performed, in early 1995, by Het Zuidelijk Toneel, based in Eindhoven, Holland. In the adaptation, which is in the main very faithful to Seneca, the Chorus is entirely omitted. The Nurse is renamed Oenone, following Racine. Hippolytus is given three companions, fellow huntsmen, who join in his initial hunting-song, and relate his death to Theseus, in place of the traditional Messenger. It has already been noted (in respect of the aside at lines 592-9) that in order to produce a performable script Claus has felt it necessary to depart somewhat from the action of the Senecan original. He does so again at the end of the play – as Garnier had done before him – by having Hippolytus' remains brought on stage in one piece in a bundle, rather than reproducing the jigsaw, so often felt to be ludicrous. Other interesting alterations will be noticed. The second act, for instance, begins in the woods, where Oenone and Phaedra have entered Hippolytus' own world to seduce him. This is a remarkable anticipation of Kragelund's suggestion for the staging of Seneca's play, described below. In Act 3 Hippolytus is still present: Theseus meets with him upon his return from the Underworld, and even summons him to answer Phaedra's charge, which he does very feebly. He is then exiled and runs off, at which point Theseus curses him for good measure. In the fourth act, Theseus announces the death of Hippolytus to Phaedra (Seneca had just left us to assume she is informed); she is remorseful and, after drinking poison, confesses her lie. The play ends with an observation from Oenone.

The most recent dramatisation of the Phaedra myth is the late Sarah Kane's *Phaedra's Love*, first performed at the Gate

Seneca: Phaedra

Theatre, London, on 15 May 1996.[21] Kane had a remarkable if brief career (she hanged herself in February of 1999) as part of the 'in-yer-face' movement; a number of her plays (but not *Phaedra's Love*, which according to her website is her least liked piece) were revived in London in 2000.

Phaedra's Love is charted through eight scenes, the first of which is an epitome of the 'in-yer-face' ethos: Hippolytus, alone in front of a television on which a violent Hollywood movie is being shown, blows his nose into a sock, and then, with nice discrimination, uses another sock to masturbate into. It is significant that this sexual act leaves him unmoved. In the next scene Phaedra unwittingly reveals her attraction to her stepson to the Doctor whom she has summoned to cure his malaise (he is bored with life, we gather). In the third scene her daughter, Strophe, is already well aware of her mother's obsession with the fat and smelly boy. It is the fourth scene that reminds us most of Seneca, for in it Phaedra personally reveals her love to her stepson, who of course rejects it. There is even a verbal reminiscence of our play when Phaedra asks Hippolytus not to address her as mother (p. 73). The source of Hippolytus' jaded appetite becomes clear in this scene: in an unexpectedly romantic touch, he has loved and lost a girl called Lena. In Scene 5 Strophe announces to her stepbrother that Phaedra has charged him with rape and killed herself (a Euripidean touch). Scene 6 puts us back on Senecan ground: Hippolytus is visited in prison by a priest, and he insists that there is no god, so that he cannot repent of any wrongdoing. In the final scene Theseus, in disguise, throws Hippolytus to a crowd clamouring for his blood. The stage directions are worthy of Seneca's most gruesome descriptive passages, since Hippolytus undergoes some terrible mutilations before he dies, cheered in his last moments nonetheless that something interesting has finally happened to him.

The play is obviously very disturbing for its nihilism, banal-

6. Reception and Later Influence

ity, violence, and foul language (all cardinal elements in the dramatic movement). What is missing in the post-Freudian world is the theme of incest, never broached, probably because a sexual relation between stepmother and stepson would not strike us as incestuous. At a stroke the most disturbing element in the traditional story is quietly removed, and in this respect Kane's is the least unsettling of all the versions of the myth of Phaedra. Still, we can see the grounds for the appeal of Seneca to a modernist sensibility, for he too chose to confront an unconventional theme as directly as his society allowed. The emotional bleakness, the isolation of the characters who scarcely engage with one another, the violence are all there in the Roman play, waiting to be transmuted into a contemporary idiom. Kane acted as a sort of catalyst upon his raw material.

7

Interpretation

In antiquity, interpretation as we know it was virtually non-existent. Scholars explained what the poet said, rather than what he might have meant. Moreover Seneca's tragedies did not become a school text, so even the most elementary sort of comment was denied them. Only with the gradual revival of interest in the mediaeval period do we begin to encounter some tentative steps towards interpretation, and as might be expected the emphasis is moral.

Nicholas Trevet (?1258-1328), the first modern commentator on Seneca's tragedies (referred to briefly above, p. 78), inherited the ancient methods of scholarship and thus largely concentrated on explaining the construction of sentences, the metres employed in the choruses, and the allusions to myth or geography. But at the outset, in his preface to the first of the plays, *Hercules Furens*, he spreads himself a bit more generously and looks at some more general issues: for example, performance. One of the things that a commentator was expected to identify was the poet's intention in writing a particular piece. (There is an example of this in Servius' brief introduction to Virgil's *Aeneid*, which doubtless served as Trevet's model.) As might be expected of a Dominican friar, Trevet perceived the intention of all Seneca's plays as ethical, the correction of moral behaviour, since literature generally was required to encourage virtue and denounce vice. The characters in a play served as examples to be followed or shunned. But Trevet never forgot that plays were also designed to amuse, and the poet's 'final cause', as he put it, using the terminology of scholastic philosophy, was 'entertainment of the audience' (*delectatio populi audientis*).[1]

Just such an entertainment was held around Christmastime, probably in 1546, when *Phaedra* was performed at Westminster School, near London. For the occasion Alexander Nowell, the headmaster (and later Dean of St Paul's Cathedral), wrote a preface in which he clarified for the audience of young boys the moral lessons to be derived from tragedy. He likens the pagan myth to the Bible story of Joseph and Potiphar's wife. Phaedra's death teaches us that great and unheard of crimes drive one to despair. He is confident that the audience will want to imitate the chaste boy and not the lewd woman. But this clarification also involved some obfuscation, since he did not make clear why Hippolytus should suffer for the viciousness of Phaedra.[2]

Senecan drama was thereafter under something of a cloud until about the middle of the last century, when re-assessment installed him more or less securely in the canon. There are therefore few critical analyses of our play until very recently. Brief mention should be made of Auguste Widal's treatise, *Sur trois tragédies de Sénèque imitées d'Euripide* (Paris, 1854), since it offered, uncharacteristically for the time, a sympathetic account of what Seneca was up to in reworking Euripidean themes. However, after Widal neglect crept back over the tragedies, until Otto Regenbogen published an important reading of Seneca's tragic corpus in 1930.[3] Its effects were somewhat slow to develop, but once it had been absorbed into the scholarly bloodstream, favourable studies of individual plays came to be more and more published. A number of the more important essays have already been mentioned in the chapters on the leading themes of the play and its literary texture. More however should here be said about the interpretation of the play as a whole in Stoic terms.

A number of scholars feel that Seneca's Stoicism animates

7. Interpretation

his poetry. Most would agree that some of the sentiments expressed in the plays are congruent with Stoic teaching, but for some that is not enough, the doctrine must be seen as integrated into the whole dramatic structure. The difficulty of this undertaking is not denied. Stoicism was characterised by its belief in divine providence, the rule of reason, and the avoidance of passion. Negate those principles and you are in the world of tragedy. Can the two be reconciled with each other? Despite the obstacles to the enterprise there are several notable attempts to demonstrate that *Phaedra* is a Stoic text, by Eckard Lefèvre, A.D. Leeman, Norman T. Pratt, and Francesco Giancotti.[4] Leeman, for example, can convincingly show that all the main characters embody a typical species of human evil; the Nurse is perhaps the most paradoxical in that she uses (as has been noted above) overtly Stoic doctrines in a bad cause (but so far as the drama goes she does not exactly herself come to a bad end). The difficulty in this analysis is that any tragic character proves to be faulty not just in Stoic terms, but in purely human terms as well. Aristotle had long before pointed to the mistakes tragic figures make; these mistakes are often born of some passion (Oedipus' anger, Hercules' lust, Creon's intransigence). One does not need to be a Stoic to see that something is amiss with the heroes of tragedy. On the other hand, there is virtually nothing in Seneca's tragedies on the positive side, and little overt urging of Stoic teaching as a corrective to the emotional and moral chaos enacted upon the stage. The moralising of the Nurse or of the Chorus in our own play is after all fairly mainstream. The Stoic readings of Senecan tragedy are often therefore lacking in cogency; recently H.M. Hine has devoted a large section of his introduction to Seneca's *Medea* to an analysis of the play in Stoic terms, and his conclusion is that a general Stoic reading of that play, at any rate, is problematic.[5] Nor does he feel that the plays generally impose a Stoic psychological reading, or that they communicate or support the physical tenets of Stoicism. This should not perhaps surprise us. No one looks for Stoicism in Seneca's satire on Claudius, the *Apocolocyntosis*. He was under no compulsion to foist it into his tragic poems either.

The most individual interpretation of our play is the late Charles Segal's *Language and Desire in Seneca's Phaedra*, a psychoanalytic reading founded chiefly upon the doctrines of Sigmund Freud as interpreted by Freud's later French follower, Jacques Lacan. An uninitiated reader is thus at once faced with a considerable impediment for lack of a fairly thorough understanding of both Freud's and Lacan's approaches to literature. Lacan moreover is a notoriously obscure and difficult writer; indeed even establishing Lacan's own position is still far from easy since he published little of his later theorising, which, in the form of seminars, was left instead to his pupils and admirers to work up into publishable form. The essential point in his psychology which Segal fixes upon is that the unconscious is structured like a language; this doctrine has an obvious appeal to the literary scholar, who feels that his own understanding of the workings of language (especially its evasions and equivocations) equips him to study the unconscious as well. But the orthodox Freudian, as Segal was aware, does not hold with this proposition, so our first ground for criticism of such an approach might well be that the foundation upon which Segal bases his reading is itself controversial, and does not command wide assent.[6]

Segal's introductory chapter, 'Language and the unconscious', thus makes considerable demands upon the reader, especially a reader who, like the present writer, knows little in general of psychoanalytic accounts of literary texts, and nothing in particular of Lacan. Segal's own reading seems to have been inspired by the impressively lucid and rigorous reading of Racine's *Phèdre* by Francesco Orlando,[7] though he rightly expresses at the outset his sense of its hazards. For many still shy

7. Interpretation

away from psychoanalytic readings of literary texts, on the grounds that they are too strictly controlled to be subjected to that sort of analysis. A student of first-century AD Latin poetry is moreover conscious that the two factors of literary influence and rhetoric are very likely to dilute the purely individual element in any text. Still, granting Segal's desire to experiment along these lines, it is surprising that Lacan's name appears so infrequently in his narrative.[8] This paucity of reference, and its confinement to footnotes, suggests no very sustained engagement with the theoretical framework Lacan is supposed to be providing for the analysis of the text. For this reason perhaps Michel David, while in general well-disposed to Segal's enterprise, regarded his reading as fundamentally impressionistic and eclectic.[9]

David's assessment rings true, since one can read the earlier portions of the book, especially the fine chapters on the imagery of landscape, the forests, the Golden Age and Nature, without being much troubled by the psychosexual underpinning (it virtually disappears much of the time). The later chapters work out the psychological implications rather more fully, yet this produces a further problem with Segal's reading of the play as a whole – its imbalance. The character he focuses upon is Hippolytus, whose hatred of women indeed seems to invite a psychological analysis. That said, his hatred is known to all (cf. lines 229-32) and exists without concealment on his part (cf. lines 555-73), so repression hardly seems to be an issue. But the tragedy is after all Phaedra's, and yet her psyche proves less open to analysis, perhaps because it is less complex. She too represses nothing, so in her case there can be no 'return of the repressed' (a Freudian doctrine that is unhelpfully never explained). She is not afraid of her father, and is unconcerned at the prospect of incest. She is the main character, yet Segal pays her much less attention than he does Hippolytus.

The reader should also be alerted to the intrusion of a contemporary sensibility which skews the interpretation. Segal is for instance among those who are unhappy about the language in which the hunt is described (pp. 60-4; this issue was touched upon above, in discussion of the characterisation of Hippolytus), and speaks of 'our' sympathy for the victims. This is insubstantial rhetoric on two counts. First, it cannot fairly be assumed that those of 'us' who eat game in the autumn have any sympathy with the pheasant and venison on 'our' plates, which undeniably met violent ends. The claim is too sweeping, even in the modern world. But, more importantly, what of antiquity? Segal never asks if a Roman's sympathy would have been evoked by the description; and rightly, for he knows that hunting was 'a favorite pastime of Seneca's contemporaries' (p. 60). So his analysis becomes a rhetorical exercise in pathos. He claims, for instance, that 'the does seek their pasture at night precisely to escape a predator like Hippolytus' (p. 61). Not only does this show ignorance of the habits of deer, it a more worrying question about the whole psychological approach to texts: if the deer's anxieties can be so mistakenly diagnosed, how accurate is the account of the human psyche likely to prove?

There are too some minor blemishes in the analysis which weaken the larger argument. At one stage Segal forgets the plot: it is not the case that Hippolytus, confronted with Phaedra, takes refuge in an idealised image of the Golden Age (so on p. 77). At that stage he has only been confronted by the Nurse, who no more than tries to soften him up; he is not replying to a disgusting proposition, but is coolly explaining, so far as he can, why the Nurse's model of behaviour does not apply to him. Segal also falls into the common error of identifying the sword with which Phaedra kills herself as Hippolytus' (see p. 30 above). Both of these lapses help to intensify the rhetoric of Segal's analysis, and it may be that his reading of the last act (especially on pp. 184-5) is compromised by Seneca's failure to specify that the sword is the same throughout.

7. Interpretation

But the chief difficulty for the general student of literature or drama with a study of this sort is the adoption of the psychoanalytic model, especially of Lacanian stamp. There is no consensus that such an approach yields valid, or valuable, analysis of the text. At the purely practical level, one has to accept that any interpretations offered in the light of Lacan's doctrine will only be acceptable to those who think they understand and believe in his model. There are moreover so few classical scholars who adopt this model that it is hard to know, for lack of comparative material, whether it is being used properly or not. On balance, then, the book's solid and undeniable merit for the general student is to be sought in the traditional assessment of the text's rich imagery; here Segal is a sure-footed guide, and, perhaps just as important, the average reader is in a position to assess the value of the analysis.

8

Performance History

It was suggested above (p. 17) that Seneca envisaged recitation as the chief medium of performance of all of his plays, at least on one occasion, though it is stoutly maintained by scholars who argue for traditional staging that recitation was only a preliminary to a performance on stage by actors. It is time now to give a brief account of what recitation entailed.[1] When the practice of reciting one's own works was introduced into Rome during the late Republic by the consul and man of letters, Gaius Asinius Pollio, its purpose above all was to secure helpful criticism from an informed and well-disposed audience that would enable a writer to improve his work before publication (which in antiquity meant copying by hand onto papyrus or parchment, and then the distribution or sale of the copies). In fact, that remained the chief function of recitation well into the first century AD and beyond; we learn this from the Letters of the Younger Pliny, who himself both attended and gave recitations (he recited his speeches and poems before publishing them).

The reciter needed first of all an auditorium, which he might have to hire or borrow from a rich friend. Seneca was rich enough to have had an auditorium of his own, perhaps, but his friends, not least the emperor, might also have provided one. Usually the author recited his own work, sitting on a platform. Now a speech, poem, or history is easily imagined being read by a single, authorial voice, but what of a play with its different parts? Here we might recall the success of Charles Dickens as a reader/performer of his novels in the nineteenth century (he was an enthusiast of the drama and keen on amateur theatricals): vast audiences across the world were held in thrall as he recited his manifold fictions.[2] We should not forget how skilful a trained actor or reader can be at producing different qualities of voice and speech. Hugh Burden or Martin Jarvis are superlative presenters of dramatic prose fiction, nicely differentiating the various parts, female as well as male. There is then no intrinsic objection to a single reader of a Senecan tragedy performing all the parts of the drama.[3] The author need not have recited in person, a trained *lector* ('reader') might on occasion be employed. There is no evidence that more than one reader was needed, and, as has been mentioned, a competent reader is quite capable of differentiating parts clearly. Dumbshow accompanying the reading is certainly attested by Pliny, Letter 9.34: he knows he reads poetry badly, so intends to hand the job over to another, and wonders what he personally is to do, accompany the reading, as others do, with gestures of hand and eye. Presumably it would have been possible to reverse the roles, and employ actors to mime the parts read by the author (though evidence for that is lacking). At any rate, one thing should be clear from this account: *recitatio* was genuine performance. It was not like silent reading at all. The speeches were properly and dramatically delivered, the odes might even have been sung (Pliny had a reader, Zosimus, who sang to the lyre [Letter 5.19]). If the reciter was any good, the effect ought to have been as electrifying as Dickens' was on his audiences.

Once the script had been recited (and perhaps revised in the light of the audience's reactions), it might be made available for copying and distribution, as is clear from the intention of Maternus in Tacitus' *Dialogus*, to publish in a revised form the play he has just recited, entitled *Cato*. But that was not the end of its performance life, even if the play was never mounted on a stage and performed by actors. As has been mentioned in the description of the *recitatio*, wealthy Romans like the younger Pliny (or

8. Performance History

like Trimalchio in Petronius' novel *Satyrica*) had trained readers, who were used at dinner parties or on other occasions to entertain the company. So the dramas could continue to be performed well after their publication. Presumably such performances would have been of excerpts, a point to bear in mind when assessing the coherence of Seneca's plots.[4]

Whatever Seneca himself intended after the initial recitation, this play has been staged, and some accounts of productions, or how to go about them are available. The earliest and most significant acted performance we know of in any detail was mounted in Rome in about 1486 by the pupils of Pomponio Leto, who was director of the Roman Academy.[5] This production was a landmark, the first Roman tragedy to be performed since antiquity. It was part of a programme for the revival of the glories of the city of old, and Leto's associates from foreign parts carried his enthusiasm back to their homelands; Erasmus mentioned it in a letter.[6] This production had a profound influence therefore upon the revival of drama after the ancient fashion. The producer was Giovanni Antonio Sulpizio of Veroli, who aspired above all to build in Rome a permanent theatre, such as he had found described in Vitruvius' treatise on architecture, which he was the first to edit for printed publication in 1486.[7] In the prefatory letter to his edition, which he dedicated to Raphael Cardinal Riaro, he pointed to the many new structures that were reviving the architectural splendour of ancient Rome (for instance the Cancelleria, commissioned by Riario), and he encouraged the cardinal to take the initiative in building a permanent theatre on the old model. He pointed to the successful revival by the 'Pomponiani' of the Roman drama in its proper form, particularly the production of *Phaedra*. He mentions interesting details: the use of a raised stage five feet high (a height derived from Vitruvius, Book 5, 6.2), an awning (which suggests the use of the courtyard of Riario's palace), the painted scenery (which may have employed the new skill of

Seneca: Phaedra

perspective drawing), and – a point surprisingly overlooked by some scholars – that the performers sang; music must have been specially written for the choral odes, an early step on the road to the creation of opera (which the handbooks tend to regard as a development of the attempt to revive Greek drama). All of these features were careful reconstructions of ancient practice: authenticity of performance is not a modern discovery. Three performances were held, one in the square before the palace of Cardinal Riario, another in the palace (probably, as suggested, in the courtyard), and a further one took place in the presence of the Holy Father in the Castel Sant'Angelo. The outdoor performance and the invitation to the people to attend indoors are particularly significant, since a public display supported by the aristocracy was also part and parcel of the attempt at revival of ancient practice, when plays were mounted for the citizens by their magistrates. The sixteen-year-old Tomaso Inghirami was so successful in the role of Phaedra that he was given that nickname ever after![8] The action was preceded by a prologue, composed by Sulpizio, which characteristically stressed that the audience would be instructed and cautioned by what it was about to witness, and that it would be alerted by warning and example (*doctior et cautior / omnis redibit, monitu et exemplo excitus*, 'everyone will go back home, wiser and more careful for having been alerted by the warning and example'). This moral note in the presentation of ancient drama is important, since it is designed to remove objections to the representation of pagan myth. It is said that the German humanist Conrad Celtis was so impressed by this performance that he had the play performed in Vienna by his students; as usual, the moral to be derived from the drama was uppermost in Celtis' mind. Back in Germany Paul Eber, a pupil of the reformer Melanchthon, mounted the play in the university town of Wittenberg in 1554.[9] (We need to remember that our play also went under the title 'Hippolytus' for a number of centuries, and,

8. Performance History

given the greater knowledge of Latin than of Greek, it is likely that unspecific references to the performance of a play of that name may well point to Seneca rather than to Euripides.)[10]

Renaissance England saw two recorded productions of *Hippolytus*, one at Westminster School, near London, probably at Christmas 1546 (its special preface was referred to above, p. 90), and the other on Shrove Tuesday, 8 February 1583 at Christ Church, Oxford.[11] This performance is especially interesting since it contains additional scenes – notably a prologue involving two divinities, composed by William Gager, who intended to enhance the purity of Hippolytus and raise his stature by having him reject a series of increasing temptations.[12] This sort of measure was necessary in the face of Puritan opposition to the stage, which was regarded, along with the players, as a nursery of immorality. It has been suggested that the choice of this play for performance was prompted by the theme of adultery, which bulked so large in mediaeval romance. Phaedra's love was something readily accessible to the contemporary audience. Still, it is somewhat odd that the Prologue states that Hippolytus pays a just penalty for rejecting women. Gager seems aware that the suffering of an entirely honourable being is unendurable.

In 1973 the Classical Society at Exeter University mounted a production of the play, and the directors published a very helpful account of their stage directions.[13] They were not trying to achieve authenticity, and so cast women in the female parts. They placed a statue of Diana on stage, since there are clear suggestions in the script that one is present (e.g. lines 405 and 424); this also served as the object of Hippolytus' devotion in the Prologue. But they also added a statue of Venus for the Chorus to address in their first song. Some of their staging required a measure of departure from what the script suggested. For instance, at lines 1109-10 parts of Hippolytus' body are brought in; this is necessary for the subsequent action but not generated at this precise point in the text. They also insist that at line 863, where Theseus orders the doors of his palace to be opened, the conversation which takes place out of doors must be imagined as happening within, an unnecessary complication. Sometimes they had to move characters on and off the stage without an indication in the script that this was to take place; this was somewhat at odds with their premise that action was always to be inferred from the script (and indeed Seneca does provide in this play a surprisingly large number of cued exits and entrances, compared to the others he wrote).

Performances of translations have also been mounted in recent decades, and some have been reviewed in the Italian periodical devoted to classical drama, *Dioniso*.[14] Ugo Albini describes a perfomance in Rome of E. Sanguineti's translation produced by Luca Ronconi in 1969: the actors were ranged in caverns upon a steeply inclined plane whence they declaimed with a minimum of movement in weird light. This undeniably privileged the verbal aspect of Senecan drama, also underscoring the isolation of the characters one from another.[15] In fact most of the productions that have been described adopt a hieratic approach to the delivery of the lines, which gives particular prominence to the words.

Another staging of an Italian translation (Faggi's) in 1981 is of particular interest, because the director, Nuccio Ladogana, undertook radical measures to render the play stageworthy, at least to modern tastes. The play opened with Phaedra dreaming of her foul ancestry; then Hippolytus is shown dreaming of the hunt. This cuts out at a stroke the juxtaposition of two long monologues. To avoid the latent comedy of the final scene, Theseus is presented as deranged by the blows that have rained down upon him after his re-emergence from the Underworld. This is undeniably an adroit expedient, but of course there is no warrant for it in the text.

The performance of a particular scene in our play is re-

8. Performance History

assessed in an engaging essay by Patrick Kragelund.[16] He argues that we should accept in principle the notion that the scene can change. This is not in itself unsatisfactory, though in general scene changes were avoided on the ancient stage, which was not enclosed on three sides as in a modern theatre. He proposes that when Phaedra says that she will be transported into the woods at line 403 the scene should indeed change to a woodland. The Nurse follows her mistress, and an altar of Diana is in the woods. This is undeniably attractive, and would give particular point to Hippolytus' anguished appeal to the woods at line 718. There is however a serious problem at line 725 where the Nurse shouts to the Athenians to render assistance to their queen. If she is in the woods, where are the Athenians? On balance, it may prove best to assume that the setting never changes, and that the action always takes place before the palace of Theseus in Athens.

9

Translations

The translation of Greek and Latin texts into the European vernaculars was one of the great literary enterprises of the Renaissance. There were many motives for translating, and one of the chief was the enrichment of the native literature by putting the model classics of antiquity into local modern dress. Thus in the mid-sixteenth century a number of translators set about creating an English Seneca. John Studley (?1545-?1590) translated four of his tragedies, and his version of *Hippolytus* (as he knew its title) was printed in *Seneca His Tenne Tragedies*.[1] B.R. Rees reckons that in many respects Studley was the least poetical of the translators whose work was collected in this volume,[2] and that his verse often descended into bathos (though it should be pointed out too that the audience plainly had a taste for a style which strikes us as sensational and bombastic). Two reasons for this are the lumbering metre employed, a fourteen-syllable line known as 'Poulter's measure', and the overworking of alliteration. Here are some examples:

> And eke the God hath tasted these whose fervent fierye handes
> The thumping thunder bouncing boltes three forded wyse doth frame.
>
> Lust favoring folly filthily did falsely forge and fayne
> Love for a God.

… his goggle eyes do glare and glister bright.

In small doses this sort of thing has a period charm, but after a page or two it is very tiresome. Not surprisingly, even in its own day this collection of translations was never reprinted, an index perhaps as much of the author's waning popularity as of the clumsiness of the translations. (Dramatic verse was making immense strides and the translations were soon antiquated by comparison to Marlowe and Shakespeare.) A few translations appeared in succeeding centuries, but there was little demand for a despised author. The situation has only been reversed within recent decades, and readers now have a considerable range of options. They will be listed now in chronological order.

Translators face an uphill task, since it is impossible for them to pinpoint a target audience for their work and produce exactly what that audience might be supposed to want. Those who are looking simply for an accurate rendering of the original are well enough served by the Loeb edition with its prose translation by Frank Justus Miller; he also equips each play with a comparative analysis setting out its similarities and differences from the Greek original (where extant).

The Penguin Classics translation by E.F. Watling is in tolerable verse; there is a substantial introduction to the volume, the text is elucidated by sparse notes, and there is an interesting appendix of Elizabethan translations (already noted).

Frederick Ahl's translation is in verse. The book has a general introduction to the series of translations of which it forms a part and a six-page introduction to *Phaedra* (referred to above in the section on characterisation). Notes are sparse but there is a very useful glossary of proper names.

The verse translation by A.J. Boyle is self-consciously stylish, indeed overpoetic for a just sense of the Senecan original, which is somehow flatter.[3] That said, the volume as a whole is very useful, since it contains an introduction (which is basically a

9. Translations

re-working of the essay referred to above, p. 114), a Latin text (the translation matches it line by line), and a commentary which is keyed to either the Latin text or the English translation.

David R. Slavitt's translation has a brief general introduction, but nothing specific on our play, nor are there any notes to explain some of the mythological allusions. His English version is avowedly (p. xv) a 'rather free approximation', designed to suggest the energy and pain of the original. But he takes freedom beyond the point at which licence begins. For instance, in Phaedra's first speech, where she refers to Theseus as the companion of Pirithous on the journey to the Underworld, Slavitt renders the single word *comes* 'companion' with two: 'his crony, his pal'. The redundancy is hardly energetic, and the linguistic register of these colloquial words (a princess of Crete is speaking) has no place in a tragedy. This jarring note is struck throughout (another example: 'Jewelry's junk!', line 387 = 391-2 of the Latin text). Another freedom the translator has permitted himself is the omission of words. Again, in this same speech, Phaedra complains that Theseus, 'the father of Hippolytus', as she says in the Latin, has gone to steal the queen of the Underworld from her husband. Now that is the first time she ever names the boy she is infatuated with, and it is given further significance because she is contrasting his farouche purity with his father's tawdry philandering. To omit the phrase 'the father of Hippolytus', as Salvitt does, arguably removes a nuance from Phaedra's character.

All of these translations are equipped with stage directions. All, however, fail, and often at the same places, to envisage a plausible *mise-en-scène*. For instance, they all have Hippolytus holding Phaedra as she speaks her give-away aside at lines 592-9, which he cannot but hear. They all lose track of movements that ought to be necessary, for instance, the problem of what, if anything, happens to Phaedra after lines 901-2, at which point if she does not exit, she must listen to Theseus' curse. True, there is no cue for an exit there, but her presence during the curse is surely gross. Likewise their directions usually do not have Theseus (or, by extension, Phaedra) exit at line 958, so they ought both to hear the Messenger's speech. The stage directions then invariably get back on the rails at line 1155, and have Phaedra enter, sword in hand. So clearly they ought after all to have had her exit at some earlier point; the translators simply have not remembered to say where. Finally, they are all alive to the problem of timing the first arrival of Hippolytus' remains on stage. Usually, despite the absence of any reference to such an action in the script, some have slaves bring on a box of body parts midway towards the end of the Messenger's speech; this is the only expedient which provides something for Phaedra to lament over in the next act (at line 1158). Others, however (Miller, Watling), do not have any of Hippolytus' remains carted on stage in the fourth act, but rather introduce them during Phaedra's fifth-act speech, just before she addresses Hippolytus at line 1168. That however is a little tardy, since Theseus has already said that she is making loud lament over a body she hates, a point at which something has to be on stage. But then they are all in difficulties at line 1247 where Theseus gets round to making the first specific reference (a command) to the arrival of the remains. What actually happens at this point is generally left unspecified.

There are also occasionally individual difficulties in charting the action; for instance, after line 583 Slavitt has the Nurse turn to the palace and see Phaedra; but he has not explained what happened to Phaedra after we saw her 'distracted, almost crazed' inside the palace at lines 385-99. Did the doors close on her, or has she been hanging around again in the background (Slavitt had Phaedra present in the background whilst Hippolytus, 'an extremely handsome, scantily clad young man', set off for the hunt in the prologue)?

9. Translations

These are all problems of stage presence and movements that cannot be easily skirted around. The translators to a man feel that these are scripts to be performed, and their directions are designed to facilitate performance. They are aware that, unusually for ancient drama, not every necessary action is generated within the script; sometimes one has to guess when something happens from the subsequent situation. And yet this effort of visualisation is not one they have made at all consistently or successfully. Much remains to be done if the action of our play is to be realised in a coherent and satisfactory way. The next translator of our play faces a considerable challenge.

Translators who aspire – as they properly should – to convey something of the flavour of Seneca's Latin have an uphill struggle, especially if their medium is modern English. Seneca was a master of Latin prose, but his verse style is much less individual.[4] What strikes a reader of the plays in their original Latin is the constant echoic buzz of earlier verse, especially that of Virgil and Ovid. Seneca knew their poems intimately and did not hesitate to frame his style upon theirs, especially the more imitable Ovid's. Now that did not necessarily rule out a measure of originality; Seneca's nephew Lucan is as indebted to the earlier masters, but despite his own youth forged an impressively individual style. Seneca, however, did not, and his lines (basically iambic in measure) are often no more than adroit reworkings of his predecessors' verses. An example in our play at lines 527-39 has been described above, where he recombines features of the Golden Age from Ovid (whose measure was basically dactylic). It smacks of a clever exercise that rarely rises however above the adroit.

Still, the language of Senecan tragedy is markedly poetic (insofar as the Romans had a poetic diction), and it is that feature especially which makes a contemporary version in English somewhat unconvincing, for modern English is virtually without a clearly poetic idiom. Here is an example: at line 434

Hippolytus, confronted by the agitated Nurse, asks if all is well with his family. In Latin his enquiry runs: *sospesque Phaedra stirpis et geminae iugum?* Literally this means: 'and is Phaedra safe, and the pair of twin offspring?' *Stirps* is a poetic word for offspring when used of particular individuals; usually it refers generally to a family's 'stock' or line. The connecting word *et* ('and') is here postponed one place from what would be its normal position before *stirpis* (a technical device called hyperbaton). Finally, the word 'iugum' is only infrequently used of two closely associated persons, because it properly means a 'yoke' of animals, oxen, say; so it is here being used metaphorically. Thus the whole expression is pretty unusual. But what is unusual about the following translations?[5]

'Phaedra safe, and their two sons?' (Miller);
'And Phaedra? And their two sons?' (Watling);
'And Phaedra safe and both their children?' (Boyle);
'Is Phaedra well? And what about the twins? Are they alright?' (Ahl).

None reproduces the slightly mannered, formal tone of Hippolytus' enquiry. Seneca presumably felt that such a tone was appropriate to tragic elevation. The modern translator can be forgiven for failing to forge out of modern English an idiom that matches this tone. But the reader who approaches Seneca without knowledge of the Latin original is undeniably deprived of something of the poetic character of his text. These are not ordinary people like us, so they were not expected talk as we would. Colloquial translations ('alright') only widen the gulf between the reader and Seneca's Latin.

Notes

1. Seneca and Roman Tragedy

1. For Seneca's life and career see Miriam T. Griffin, *Seneca, a Philosopher in Politics* (Oxford: Clarendon Press, 1976); those with less stamina can read her shorter essay in C.D.N. Costa (editor), *Seneca* (London & Boston: Routledge & Kegan Paul, 1974), pp. 1-38.

2. There is no monograph in English dedicated to Seneca as philosopher, but for Stoicism generally see R.W. Sharples, *Stoics, Epicureans and Sceptics: an Introduction to Hellenistic Philosophy* (London & New York: Routledge, 1996), and for Seneca's Stoicism F.H. Sandbach, *The Stoics* (Ancient Culture and Society; London: Chatto & Windus, 1975), pp. 149-62, or John M. Cooper and J.F. Procopé, *Seneca, Moral and Political Essays* (Cambridge: Cambridge University Press, 1995), pp. xvi-xxvi.

3. In his *Institutio oratoria* 'Educating the Orator', 10.1.125-31, he provides an extended but critical appreciation of Seneca's talent as a prose writer; he ignores his poetry completely.

4. For the tradition of the Latin pointed style, and of Seneca's place in it, the best account remains the introduction by Walter Coventry Summers to *Select Letters of Seneca* (London: Macmillan & Co., 1910; often reprinted).

5. The literary character of the period is discussed by R.G. Mayer, 'Neronian Classicism', *American Journal of Philology* 103 (1983), pp. 305-18. For Nero as performer and the genres of theatrical expression current in his day see R.C. Beacham, *Spectacle Entertainments of Early Imperial Rome* (New Haven & London: Yale University Press, 1999), pp. 210-37.

6. 'Sense Pauses and Relative Dating in Seneca, Sophocles and Shakespeare', *American Journal of Philology* 102 (1981), pp. 289-307. These issues are reviewed by Michael Coffey, Introduction to M. Coffey and R. Mayer (editors), *Seneca: Phaedra* (Cambridge Greek and Latin Classics; Cambridge: Cambridge University Press, 1990), pp. 3-5.

7. For example, Eckard Lefèvre's view that the Nurse's speech at

Notes to pages 9-21

204-17 hints at the death of Agrippina, which took place in 59, is rendered untenable; 'Die politische Bedeutung von Senecas *Phaedra*', *Wiener Studien* 24 (1990), pp. 109-22, especially p. 117.

8. On this see L.A. Mackay, 'The Roman Tragic Spirit', in *California Studies in Classical Antiquity* 8 (1975), pp. 145-62.

9. See J.G. Fitch, 'Playing Seneca?', in G.W.M. Harrison (editor), *Seneca in Performance* (London: Duckworth / Classical Presss of Wales, 2000), p. 7.

10. The articles 'mime' and 'pantomime' in the *OCD* give helpful orientation.

11. At Rome important poets, for instance Seneca's nephew Lucan, and later Statius, wrote pantomime scripts (Lucan is credited with fourteen).

12. S.M. Goldberg, 'The Fall and Rise of Roman Tragedy', *Transactions of the American Philological Association* 126 (1996), p. 276.

13. This point is stressed by Elaine Fantham, 'Production of Seneca's *Trojan Women,* Ancient? and Modern', in Harrison, *Seneca in Performance*, p. 22. See also Victoria Tietze Larson, *The Role of Description in Senecan Tragedy* (Frankfurt, etc.: Peter Lang, 1994), p. 55.

14. Goldberg, 'Fall', p. 283 n. 21.

15. Gordon Williams has noted how the speakers in Senecan tragedy tend to address themselves over the heads of the others on stage to the audience directly; he does not specify that this might be characteristic of recitation, but it certainly suits recitation better than traditional staged drama; 'Poet and Audience in Senecan Tragedy: *Phaedra* 358-430' in T. Woodman and J. Powell (editors), *Author and Audience in Latin Literature* (Cambridge: Cambridge University Press, 1992), pp. 138-49.

16. A case for reading as intrinsically superior to staging is made by Don Fowler in 'Reading Senecan Tragedy', in *Unrolling the Text: Books and Readers in Roman Poetry* (Oxford: Oxford University Press, 2002). My friend and colleague Professor Alessandro Schiesaro kindly permitted me to see this valuable discussion before its publication.

2. The Action of the Play

1. Ovid in his poem on antidotes for love, *Remedia Amoris*, had recommended hunting as a displacement activity for the lovelorn, lines 200-10. As he noted, you'll be too tired to have time for love-making.

2. Some argue for its thematic importance in the play, but that of course is another issue.

3. The prologue is given an allegorical reading by F. Zoccali, 'Il prologo "allegorico" della Phaedra di Seneca', *Bolletino di Studi Latini* 27 (1997), pp. 433-53, with a résumé on p. 453: the hunt suggests

Notes to pages 21-37

pursuit of a non-responsive beloved, and that prepares us for what is to come.

4. See C. Lazzarini, *Ovidio: Rimedi contro l'Amore* (Venice: Marsilio, 1986), pp. 140-1.

5. It needs to be said at this point that I am here assuming the distribution of speeches as set out in my own edition of 1990; most translators follow earlier editors, and attribute the prayer to the Nurse herself.

6. See Charles Segal, 'Dissonant Sympathy: Song, Orpheus and the Golden Age in Seneca's Tragedies' in A.J. Boyle (editor), *Seneca Tragicus* (Berwick: Aureal Publications, 1983), pp. 244-9, M.G. Critelli, 'L'Arcadia impossibile: elementi di un'età dell'oro nella *Phaedra* di Seneca', *Rivista di cultura classica e medioevale* 40 (1998), pp. 71-6, and C. Maxia, 'Seneca e l'età d'oro', *Bolletino di Studi Latini* 30 (2000), pp. 87-105, especially 98-100 for our play.

7. Euripides left two plays on the theme, the earlier, and now lost, *Hippolutos Kaluptomenos*, 'Hipploytus Veiled', and the extant *Hippolutos Stephanephoros*, 'Hippolytus with the Garland'. Seneca knew and used both, as we shall see.

8. Of course it is conceivable that in the first Hippolytus play Euripides had Phaedra send the young man a note by the Nurse, but he will not have needed to read the note out loud to the audience in order to convey its contents: his shocked reaction will have sufficed.

9. The interpretation offered of this scene was first propounded by Ugo Moricca, 'Le fonti della *Fedra* di Seneca', *Studi italiani di filologia classica* 21 (1915), pp. 158-224, and revived by Pierre Grimal, 'L'originalité de Sénèque dans la tragédie de Phèdre', *Revue des Études Latines* 41 (1963), pp. 297-314 (= *Rome: la littérature et l'histoire* (Rome: École française de Rome, 1986), i.557-73).

10. For the importance of disclosure in Racine's play and his particular debt to Seneca's scene see Martin Mueller, *Children of Oedipus and Other Essays on the Imitation of Greek Tragedy, 1550-1800* (Toronto: University of Toronto Press, 1980), pp. 47-9.

11. There is an analysis of this scene by Francesco Caviglia, 'La morte di Ippolito nella *Fedra* di Seneca', *Quaderni di Cultura e di Tradizione Classica* 8 (1990), pp. 119-33.

12. D.F. Sutton, *Seneca on the Stage* (Leiden: E.J. Brill, 1986), pp. 52-3.

13. M. Coffey, Introduction to Coffey and Mayer (editors), *Seneca: Phaedra*, p. 16.

3. The Major Themes of the Play

1. Nature is a much-discussed topic in the drama: see Peter J. Davis, '*Vindicat Omnes Natura Sibi*: a Reading of Seneca's *Phaedra*' in

Notes to pages 37-42

Boyle, *Seneca Tragicus*, pp. 114-27, A.J. Boyle, 'In Nature's Bonds: a Study of Seneca's *Phaedra*', in H. Temporini (editor), *Aufstieg und Niedergang der römischen Welt* II 32.2 (Berlin & New York: De Gruyter, 1985), 1284-347, and M.G. Critelli, 'Ideologia e simbologia della natura nella *Phaedra* di Seneca', *Rivista di cultura classica e medioevale* 41 (1999), pp. 233-43. Chapter 4 of Segal, *Language and Desire*, is also useful, especially for the bibliographical references.

2. It should be noted however that the great Stoic teacher Chrysippus had regarded incest as 'natural', in that animals practise it (see Plutarch's *On Stoic Self-Contradictions* 22 in the Loeb Classical Library edition [Cambridge, MA: Harvard University Press, 1976], xiii.2, pp. 506-7).

3. A Freudian study of incest in literature is offered by Otto Rank, *The Incest Theme in Literature and Legend* (Baltimore: Johns Hopkins University Press, 1992); this is a translation by Gregory C. Richter of a work which appeared in German in 1912. It refers briefly to Seneca's treatment of the Phaedra Scheme (as Rank called it) on p. 128. The psychoanalytic approach was revived by Segal, *Language and Desire*. There is also a chapter on incest in Antonella Borgo's *Lessico parentale in Seneca tragico* (Naples: Loffredo, 1993), pp. 38-51, especially pp. 49-51 on our play. Her whole volume is relevant to the wider topic of the deployment of words specifying family relationships to enhance tragic pathos.

4. The third topic I have in mind is a father killing his sons, the theme of the *Hercules Furens*.

5. See M.R. Rivoltella, 'Il motivo della colpa ereditaria nelle tragedie senecane: una ciclicità in "crescendo" ', *Aevum* 67 (1993), pp. 113-28.

6. Segal, *Language and Desire*, p. 35 n. 10 offers ample bibliography for the discussion of the Minotaur and Phaedra's heredity. The bull imagery of the play as a whole, some of which reinforces the heredity theme, is charted by Michael Paschalis, 'The Bull and the Horse: Animal Theme and Imagery in Seneca's *Phaedra*', *American Journal of Philology* 115 (1994), pp. 105-28, esp. 105-8.

7. But Seneca has somewhat forgotten himself at this point, since at line 226 the Amazon Antiope was said to be chaste by the Nurse.

8. In Euripides' play Hippolytus is a bastard.

9. Further examples of this juxtaposition will be seen in lines 948, 998, 1251-2, 1272.

10. There is a first-rate account of madness in Seneca by H.M. Hine in his commentary on Seneca's *Medea* 139-40 (Warminster: Aris & Phillips, 2000), p. 133. For the universality of *furor* in our play see D. Henry and B. Walker, 'Phantasmagoria and Idyll: an Element of Seneca's *Phaedra*', *Greece and Rome* 13 (1966), pp. 223-9, Regina Fucito Merzlak, '*Furor* in Seneca's *Phaedra*', in C. Deroux (editor),

Studies in Latin Literature and Roman History (Collection Latomus 180; Brussels: Latomus, 1983), iii.193-210, and Coffey, Introduction to Coffey and Mayer, *Seneca: Phaedra*, p. 26.

11. But see Bernard Williams, *Shame and Necessity* (Berkeley & London: University of California Press, 1993), p. 149, with the articles referred to in n. 37 on p. 213.

12. This view has been recently controverted by Hanna M. Roisman, *Nothing is as it Seems: the Tragedy of the Implicit in Euripides' Hippolytus* (Lanham, MD & Oxford: Rowman & Littlefield, 1999).

4. Characterisation

1. This is a somewhat off-the-cuff observation on his part, since Stoic theory regarded the sexes as possessing equal capacity for moral action, a view Seneca himself endorses in *Dialogue* 6.16.1. See now R. Gazich, 'La *Fedra* di Seneca tra *pathos* ed elegia', *Humanitas (Brescia)* 52 (1997), pp. 348-75.

2. See his edition of Euripides' *Hippolytos* (Oxford: Clarendon Press, 1964), p. 36.

3. For this see E. Vernon Arnold, *Roman Stoicism* (Cambridge: Cambridge University Press, 1911), pp. 270-1.

4. Seneca himself contrasts the healthy hunger of the hunter with the queasiness of the pampered in Letter 95.18. At *Aeneid* 9.605 hunting is said to be a characteristic of the primitive youth of Italy.

5. The similar biblical tale of Joseph and Potiphar's wife is found in Genesis 39:7-20; the handsome Bellerophon repelled the advances of Anteia or Sthenobaea (depending on the version of the myth), who in pique denounced him to her husband Proteus. This myth was the subject of a Euripidean tragedy.

6. 'A New Look at Seneca's *Phaedra*', in Harrison, *Seneca in Performance*, pp. 73-86. She relies heavily upon a contrast with Euripides' extant play, as interpreted in her monograph on it (see above, Chapter 3 n. 12).

7. The Nurse's broader function, rather than character, is given a vast philosophical dimension by Jens Uwe Schmidt, 'Phaedra und der Einfluss ihrer Amme: zum Sieg des mythischen Weltbildes über die Philosophie in Senecas *Phaedra*', *Philologus* 139 (1995), pp. 274-323.

5. Literary Texture

1. This point is made by Harry Hine in *Journal of Roman Studies* 77 (1987), p. 257, and reiterated by R.J. Tarrant, 'Greek and Roman in Seneca's Tragedies', in C.P. Jones, C. Segal, R.J. Tarrant, R.F. Thomas (editors), *Greece in Rome: Influence, Integration, Resistance* (Harvard

Studies in Classical Philology 97) (Cambridge, MA: Harvard University Press, 1995), pp. 216, 219.

2. The relationship between Seneca and Euripides is discussed by Segal, *Language*, pp. 202-14; a more systematic comparative analysis, though somewhat superficial, is provided by Hans Jürgen Tschiedel, 'La *Fedra* di Seneca: una lettura', *Aevum Antiquum* 10 (1997), pp. 337-53.

3. It must be emphasised that we simply do not know precisely what gave rise to the audience's disapproval of the first Hippolytus play. W.S. Barrett, for instance, is not alone in suggesting that Phaedra made her approach to Hippolytos in person, but there is not a shred of evidence for this speculation. Phaedra would have been shameless enough by Greek male standards if she had simply set out to seduce her stepson through the agency of the Nurse, as I have just suggested.

4. It seems immaterial that the action is set by Seneca in Athens, following presumably the first Euripidean version, rather than Troezen, as in the second.

5. M. Coffey, Introduction to Coffey and Mayer, *Seneca: Phaedra*, p. 28.

6. 'Virgil's Dido and Seneca's Tragic Heroines', *Greece and Rome* 22 (1975), pp. 1-10.

7. For a discussion of this borrowing see J.J. Gahan, '*Imitatio* and *Aemulatio* in Seneca's *Phaedra*', *Latomus* 46 (1987), pp. 380-7. He suggests that Seneca himself invented the re-assembly of Hippolytus' body in an effort to rival Euripides.

8. There is a detailed discussion of an earlier example of the Nurse's Ovidian advice and the 'plurivocity' of the possible readings it evokes by Mireille Armisen-Marchetti, 'Pour une lecture des tragédies de Sénèque. L'exemple de *Phèdre*, v. 130-135', *Pallas* 38 (1992), pp. 379-90. There is a résumé in English on p. 390.

9. G.O. Hutchinson offers a suave reading of his whole speech in *Latin Literature from Seneca to Juvenal* (Oxford: Clarendon Press, 1993), pp. 160-4.

10. I discuss this feature of Senecan writing in 'Doctus Seneca', *Mnemosyne* 43 (1990), pp. 395-407.

6. Reception and Later Influence

1. There is a text and translation with notes in the Loeb Classical Library edition of Prudentius by H.J. Thomson (Cambridge, MA: Harvard University Press, 1953), ii.304-23. See also A.-M. Palmer, *Prudentius on the Martyrs* (Oxford: Clarendon Press, 1989), pp. 188-93, especially pp. 189-90 n. 30, and M.J. Roberts, *Poetry and the Cult of the Martyrs: the Liber Peristephanon of Prudentius* (Ann Arbor: University of Michigan Press, 1993), pp. 153-67, especially p. 155 n. 50

for Seneca's influence on Prudentius, and p. 156 n. 52 for the one difference. There are further discussions of the poets by F. Gasti, 'La "passione" di Ippolito: Seneca e Prudenzio', *Quaderni di Cultura e di Tradizione Classica* 11 (1993), pp. 215-28, W. Evenpoel, 'Le martyre dans le Peristephanon Liber de Prudence', *Sacris Erudiri* 36 (1996), pp. 5-35, and P.-A. Deproost, 'Le martyre chez Prudence: sagesse et tragédie. La reception de Sénèque dans le Peristephanon Liber', *Philologus* 143 (1999), pp. 161-80 .

2. See the article on 'Hippolytus' in the *Lexicon Iconographicum Mythologiae Classicae* (Zurich & Munich: Artemis, 1990), i.449-60 (especially p. 460 for references to scenes that possibly show Senecan influence on the presentation of the myth), and also Coffey, Introduction to Coffey and Mayer, *Seneca: Phaedra*, p. 33, and P. Ghiron-Bistagne, 'Il motivo di Fedra nell'iconografia e la *Fedra* di Seneca', *Dioniso* 52 (1985), pp. 261-306.

3. There is a good discussion of the relation between the works by G.J.P. O'Daly, *The Poetry of Boethius* (London: Duckworth, 1991), pp. 127-31. A more general discussion of Boethius' use of Seneca is found in Appendix 1 'Seneca's Plays in the *Consolation of Philosophy*' of Seth Lerer's *Boethius and Dialogue: Literary Method in the Consolation of Philosophy* (Princeton: Princeton University Press, 1985), pp. 237-53, especially pp. 239-40.

4. See R.J. Tarrant in L.D. Reynolds (editor), *Texts and Transmission: a Survey of the Latin Classics* (Oxford: Clarendon Press, 1986 corrected edition), pp. 378-81.

5. There are two general studies of these playwrights – neither of which I have seen – by Daniela Dalla Valle, *Gli 'Hippolytes' senechiani del teatro francese* (Turin, 1986), and *Quando Ippolito s'innamora* (Turin, 1990). Indebted to them is a shorter essay by G. Garbarino, 'La Fedra di Seneca e alcune tragedie francesi del Seicento', *Quaderni di Cultura e di Tradizione Classica* 19 (1992), pp. 277-89.

6. Garnier's *Hippolyte* has been edited by Raymond Lebègue (Paris: Société Les Belles Lettres, 1974), who discusses on pp. 237-45 his sources and on p. 251 his particular debts to Seneca, and by C.M. Hill and M.G. Morrison (London: Athlone Press, 1975), who devote pp. 10-13 to sources and structure. See also E. Lefèvre, *Der Einfluss Senecas auf das europäische Drama* (Darmstadt: Wissenschaftliche Buchgesellschaft, 1978), pp. 187-90. There are many critical comparisons of Garnier and Seneca, and a convenient one in English is by V.C. Barsan, *Garnier and Seneca* (Dissertation, University of Illinois, 1965, published by University Microfilms in 1965), pp. 143-84; most helpful is the essay by Peter Davis, 'Rewriting Seneca: Garnier's *Hippolyte*', in *Classical and Modern Literature* 17.4 (1997), pp. 293-318; he offers a full recent bibliography in n. 1.

7. La Pinelière's *Hippolyte* is discussed by Winifred Newton, *Le*

Thème de Phèdre et d'Hippolyte dans la littérature française (Paris: E. Droz, 1939), pp. 36-45 (she also deals with Garnier and Racine), and in Lefèvre, *Einfluss*, p. 190.

8. Cornelius Jansen (1585-1638), bishop of Ypres, had tried in his teaching, embodied in the posthumously published *Augustinus*, to revitalise Roman Catholicism by enhancing its spiritual (rather than dialectic or ceremonial) dimension. He emphasised man's sinfulness and utter dependence upon his love of God, a love he may be born with or only acquire through conversion (a process itself dependent upon God's will). This stressed the importance of the direct relation between man and God (a Protestant tenet), and produced in its adherents a measure of introspective uncertainty. William Doyle, *Jansenism: Catholic Resistance to Authority from the Reformation to the French Revolution* (Studies in European History; Basingstoke: Macmillan, 2000) offers a helpful orientation to the history of the movement.

9. R.W. Tobin, *Racine and Seneca* (Chapel Hill: University of North Carolina Press, 1971), p. 131 n. 1.

10. But the opposing aspects of the heroine's character highlighted by the two authors are noted by Philippe Heuzé, 'Les aveux de Phèdre', in R. Chevalier and R. Poignault (editors), *Présence de Sénèque* (Paris: Touzot, 1991), pp. 171-8.

11. Jean Pommier, *Aspects de Racine* (Paris: Librairie Nizet, 1954), p. 187.

12. John Lapp, *Aspects of Racinian Tragedy* (Toronto: University of Toronto Press, 1955), pp. 170-9.

13. See p. 69 of M. Autrand's French school edition of the play in the Nouveaux Classiques Larousse series (Paris: Librairie Larousse, 1971), or pp. 136-7 of a similar edition by X. Darcos in the Classiques Hachette series (Paris: Hachette Livre, 1991). These editions, by the way, provide ample coverage of Racine's debt to Seneca.

14. Further discussion of the characterisation of Phèdre will be found in Edward James and Gillian Jondorf, *Racine: Phèdre* (Landmarks of World Literature, Cambridge: Cambridge University Press, 1994), pp. 61-9.

15. The narration is carefully analysed by Lapp, *Aspects of Racinian Tragedy*, pp. 164-7, and is more briefly discussed by Tobin, *Racine and Seneca*, pp. 137-9.

16. For further discussion of Racine see Lefèvre, *Einfluss*, pp. 126, 211-20; J.M. Osho, 'Variations on the Phaedra Theme in Euripides, Seneca and Racine', in *Nigeria and the Classics* 12 (1970), pp. 86-101; Coffey, Introduction to Coffey and Mayer, *Seneca: Phaedra*, pp. 34-5.

17. See Coffey, Introduction, pp. 39-40.

18. For D'Annunzio there is a collective volume entitled *Fedra da Euripide a D'Annunzio, Quaderni dannunziani* 5-6 (1989). The relevant essay is by F. Giancotti, 'Profilo della *Fedra* di Seneca con raffronti dannunziani specie in rapporto al finale', pp. 51-75, esp. p. 68. There is also a study by E. Paratore, 'La morte di Fedra in Seneca e nel D'Annunzio', in V. Gabrieli (editor), *Friendship's Garland. Essays ... Mario Praz* (Rome, 1966), pp. 413-34.

19. Claus' *Phaedra (naar Seneca)* was published in 1995 (Amsterdam: International Theatre and Film Books). For an English-language website on Claus, which refers to others in Flemish, see: http://www.kirjasto.sci.fi/hclaus.htm. My friend Dr Vincent Hunink has kindly provided me with notice of the following discussions of Claus' use of the Phaedra myth: Paul Claes, *De mot zit in de mythe* (Amsterdam, 1984), pp. 297-306; Rudi van der Paardt, *Antieke motieven in de moderne Nederlandse letterkunde, een eigentijdse Odyssee* (Amsterdam, 1982), pp. 78-97; Rudi van der Paardt, *Mythe en metamorfose, klassieke themas en motieven in de moderne literatuur* (Amsterdam, 1991), pp. 147-72.

20. His views are recorded by Paul Claes, *Claus-reading* (Amsterdam, 1984), p. 85. Again, my thanks to Dr Hunink for this valuable observation.

21. *Phaedra's Love* was published in the series Methuen Modern Plays (London: Methuen, 1996). Kane's website is at: http://www.iainfisher.com/kane.html. The theatre-movement is described by Aleks Sierz, *In Yer Face Theatre: British Drama Today* (London: Faber & Faber, 2001), who of course discusses Kane's work; he also wrote about her in the *Daily Telegraph* (27 May 2000), p. A1. There is a website for the movement: http://www.inyerface-theatre.com/credits.html.

7. Interpretation

1. For Trevet see Roland Mayer, 'Personata Stoa: Neostoicism and Senecan Tragedy', *Journal of the Warburg and Courtauld Institutes* 57 (1994), pp. 154-5, S. Marchitelli, 'Nicholas Trevet und die Renaissance der Senecas Tragoedien', *Museum Helveticum* 56 (1999), pp. 36-63, 87-104, and Franco Caviglia, 'Commenti di ecclesiastici a Seneca Tragico: Trevet e Delrio', *Aevum Antiquum* 13 (2000), pp. 351-63. Trevet's commentary on the *Phaedra* exists still only in MS, e.g. Bodley 292 and Soc. Antiq. 63 (others have been published). The latter is briefly described by Pamela J. Willetts in the *Catalogue of the Manuscripts in the Society of Antiquaries of London* (London: D.S. Brewer for the Society, 2000), p. 30. I am grateful to the Society and to their Librarian, Mr Bernard Nurse, for allowing me to read the MS.

2. On Nowell's preface for the 1546 performance in Westminster School see B.R. Smith, *Ancient Scripts and Modern Experience on the English Stage 1500-1700* (Princeton: Princeton University Press, 1988), p. 202.

Notes to pages 90-99

3. 'Schmerz und Tod in den Tragödien Senecas', *Vorträge der Bibliothek Warburg 1927-1928* (1930), pp. 167-218.
4. Eckard Lefèvre, *'Quid ratio possit?* Senecas *Phaedra* als stoisches Drama', *Wiener Studien* 3 (1969), pp. 131-60 (= Eckard Lefèvre (editor), *Senecas Tragödien* [Wege der Forschung 310; Darmstadt: Wissenschaftliche Buchgesellschaft, 1972], pp. 343-75); A.D. Leeman, 'Seneca's *Phaedra* as a Stoic tragedy', in J.M. Bremer, S.L. Radt and C.J. Ruijgh (editors), *Miscellanea Tragica in Honorem J.C. Kamerbeek* (Amsterdam: A. Hakkert, 1976), pp. 199-212; Norman T. Pratt, *Seneca's Drama* (Chapel Hill & London: University of North Carolina Press, 1983), pp. 91-6; Francesco Giancotti, *Poesia e filosofia in Seneca tragico, la Fedra* (Turin: CELID, 1986).
5. *Seneca's Medea* (Warminster: Aris & Phillips, 2000), pp. 27-30.
6. The difficulties thrown up by Lacan's writing and theorising, as well as his heterodoxy, are sharply analysed by Malcolm Bowie, *Lacan* (Cambridge, MA & London: Harvard University Press, 1991), a book to which I owe my own superficial grasp of the issues at stake. The fragility of Segal's position is the chief target of the extended review by Franco Caviglia in *Aevum* 65 (1991), pp. 183-7.
7. *Toward a Freudian Theory of Literature* (Baltimore & London: Johns Hopkins University Press, 1978). Orlando repudiates the autobiographical use of texts for psychological analysis of the author; it is odd therefore that Segal is prepared to entertain on pp. 58-9 the notion that Seneca's own unconscious desires and unsublimated sexual energies are engaged in sympathy for Phaedra.
8. To the scanty references listed in the Index may be added those on pp. 119 n. 10, 136 n. 14, 140 n. 20, and 142 n. 24.
9. 'Mito e tragedie di Fedra nella letteratura psicanalitica', *Quaderni dannunziani* 5-6 (1989), pp. 22-3.

8. Performance History

1. The fullest collection of the evidence remains the extensive note on Juvenal *Satire* 3.9 by J.E.B. Mayor (London & New York: Macmillan, 1889), i.173-82. The article 'recitation' in *OCD* is also helpful.
2. See Paul Schlicke (editor), *Oxford Reader's Companion to Dickens* (Oxford: Oxford University Press, 1999) s.v. 'public readings'.
3. It is also worth recalling that the pantomime dancer also performed alone, and might impersonate anything up to five different characters in a single piece. Such adaptability was part of the skill.
4. See H.A. Kelly, 'Tragedy and the Performance of Tragedy in Late Roman Antiquity', in *Traditio* 35 (1979), pp. 21-44.
5. Information on this famous Roman performance was first collected by Fortunato Pintor, *Rappresentazioni romane di Seneca e Plauto nel Rinascimento* (Perugia, 1906), a book I have not seen; the

documents are reprinted with German translations in W.M.A. Creizenach's valuable *Geschichte des neueren Dramas* (Halle: Max Niemeyer, 1918, 2nd edition), ii.346-7. Margret Dietrich, 'Pomponius Laetus Wiederentdeckung des antiken Theaters', in *Maske und Kothurn* 3 (1957), pp. 245-67, esp. pp. 256-7 and Smith (*Ancient Scripts*, pp. 3-5) stress the new epoch in drama production initiated by this Rome performance.

6. Erasmus' reference to it – admittedly many years after the event – is in Letter no. 1347, which is translated by R.A.B. Mynors in *The Collected Works of Erasmus: Correspondence* (Toronto, Buffalo, London: University of Toronto Press, 1989), ix.421.

7. Sulpizio's preface to Vitruvius and his Prologue to *Phaedra* (among other documents) are now most conveniently found with Italian translations in Fabrizio Cruciani, *Teatro nel Rinascimento: Roma 1450-1550* (Rome: Bulzoni, 1983), pp. 219-27. The third volume of P.G. Bietenholz and T.B. Deutscher (editors), *Contemporaries of Erasmus: a Biographical Register of the Renaissance and Reformation* (Toronto, Buffalo & London: University of Toronto Press, 1986), contains accounts of Riario by D.S. Chambers (iii.153-4) and of Sulpizio by Judith Rice Henderson (iii.300).

8. Danilo Aguzzi-Barbagli has an article on Inghirami, who became Vatican librarian, in Bietenholz and Deutscher, *Contemporaries of Erasmus*, ii.223-5.

9. Information on performances in Renaissance Germany is derived from W. Trillitzsch, 'Seneca tragicus – Nachleben und Beurteilung im lateinischen Mittelalter von der Spätantike bis zum Renaissancehumanismus', in *Philologus* 122 (1978), pp. 134-5. Many other writers' acquaintance with the plays generally is listed in this helpful article.

10. There is notice of a production in France in 1474 in the palace of the cardinal Saint-Georges, a nephew of Sixtus IV, in Howard Lee Nostrand, *Le théâtre antique et à l'antique en France de 1840 à 1900* (Paris: E. Droz, 1934), p. 12, supported by reference to Ch. Magnin, *Revue des Deux Mondes*, 1 June 1844, 898-900. This may be accurate but for the date: Riario (who was Cardinal of the title of Saint George and a great-nephew of Sixtus) went into exile in France from 1492 to 1503, during the pontificate of Alexander VI (Borgia). Perhaps then the date in question is 1494. It would be interesting to know more about this, since Riario seems to be trying to revive a success.

J. Jacquot gives an unsupported reference to a performance in Ferrara in 1509 in 'Sénèque, La Renaissance et nous', in J. Jacquot (editor), *Les Tragédies de Sénèque et le théâtre de la Renaissance* (Paris: Centre National pour la Recherche Scientifique, 1964), p. 281, which he may have derived from the article on Seneca in the *Enciclopedia dello Spettacolo* (Rome: Le Maschere, 1961), viii.1835.

11. Performances in Renaissance England are discussed by F.S.

Boas, *University Drama in the Tudor Age* (Oxford: Clarendon Press, 1914), pp. 197-201 (for Gager's version), and Smith, *Ancient Scripts*, pp. 199-205 for the 1546 performance in Westminster School, and pp. 211-15 for the Christ Church staging.

12. The expanded script used on that occasion and the controversy that it evoked is described by J.W. Binns, 'William Gager's Additions to Seneca's *Hippolytus*', in *Studies in the Renaissance* 17 (1970), pp. 153-91.

13. The Exeter University production is described by S. Fortey and J. Glucker, 'Actus Tragicus: Seneca on the Stage', *Latomus* 34 (1975), pp. 699-715. Some original material relating to the production is in the Oxford Archive.

14. For accounts of some of the recent Italian (and other) stagings see C. Barone, 'Un recente allestimento della *Fedra* di Seneca', *Dioniso* 52 (1981), pp. 449-53 (Ladogana's), R. Trombino, 'Phaedra on the stage: sul recente allestimento della *Phaedra* di Seneca a cura di Franco Ricordi', *Dioniso* 58 (1988), pp. 137-40, and the useful account of stagings of Senecan tragedy generally by F. Amoroso, 'Messa in scena di Seneca tragico', *Dioniso* 63.2 (1993), pp. 87-100. He knows of some nine modern stagings, and describes on pp. 92-3 Luca Ronconi's Rome production of 1969. Finally, A. Andrisano, *Fedra*, *Dioniso* 65.1-2 (1995), pp. 90-3, gives some account of the staging of scenes from various Phaedra-dramas in Bologna in 1995.

15. See *Atti delle giornate di studio su Fedra*, p. 139 (= *Viaggio nel teatro classico* [Florence: Le Monnier, 1987], pp. 146-54).

16. 'Senecan Tragedy: Back on Stage?', *Classica et Mediaevalia* 50 (1999), pp. 239-43.

9. Translations

1. This was reprinted for the Tudor Translations series (London: Constable & Co., 1927), and was introduced in a famous essay by T.S. Eliot, 'Seneca in Elizabethan Translation', itself reprinted in his *Selected Essays* (London: Faber & Faber, 1961), pp. 65-105.

2. 'English Seneca: a Preamble', *Greece and Rome* 16 (1969), p. 123. Selections from Studley's translation are to be found in Don Share (editor), *Seneca in English* (Harmondsworth: Penguin, 1998), pp. 28-45 and in Appendix I of Watling's Penguin Classics translation.

3. Elaine Fantham, a notable student of Senecan drama, criticises it for its 'mannered and unpleasing verse' in *Quaderni di Cultura e di Tradizione Classica* 11 (1993), p. 161.

4. If his verse had impressed the Romans as much as his prose plainly did Quintilian could not have failed to draw attention to it in his famous list of classic authors to be imitated in the tenth book of his *Institutio oratoria*.

Notes to page 110

5. Slavitt's version is omitted, since, as already noted, he makes no attempt to transpose the Senecan tragic register into contemporary English.

Guide to Further Reading

Texts, translations and commentaries

L. Annaei Senecae Tragoediae, edited by F. Leo (Berlin: Weidmann, 1879). The first volume contains valuable essays (*Observationes*, written in Latin) on Senecan drama.

L. Annaei Senecae Tragoediae, edited by O. Zwierlein (Oxford Classical Text; Oxford, 1986). Critical – and now standard – edition of the Latin text; reprints contain additional matter in the *Praefatio*.

Michael Coffey and Roland Mayer (editors), *Seneca: Phaedra* (Cambridge Greek and Latin Classics: Cambridge: Cambridge University Press, 1990).

F. Ahl, *Seneca. Three Tragedies* (Ithaca & London: Cornell University Press, 1986).

A.J. Boyle, *Seneca's Phaedra* (Latin and Greek Texts, 5; Liverpool: Francis Cairns, 1987).

Frank Justus Miller, *Seneca Tragedies* (Loeb Classical Library; Cambridge, MA: Harvard University Press, 1917). Reprints Leo's Latin text with a prose translation. Miller also produced a verse translation (Chicago: University of Chicago Press, 1907), reprinted in G.E. Duckworth (editor), *The Complete Roman Drama* (New York: Random House, 1942), vol. 2.

David R. Slavitt in David R. Slavitt and Palmer Bovie (editors), *Seneca, The Tragedies*, vol. 1 (Complete Roman Drama in Translation; Baltimore & London: Johns Hopkins University Press, 1992).

E.F. Watling, *Seneca: Four Tragedies and Octavia* (Harmondsworth: Penguin, 1966).

General books and articles on Seneca and Roman tragedy

OCD: *Oxford Classical Dictionary*, edited by S. Hornblower and A. Spawforth, 3rd edition (Oxford: Oxford University Press, 1996), is an indispensable handbook, and provides solid orientation on matters of myth, authors, and literary terms.

Seneca: Phaedra

W. Beare, *The Roman Stage*[3] (London: Methuen & Co. Ltd., 1964). Provides a still useful store of information on all aspects of drama at Rome.

R.J. Tarrant, 'Senecan drama and its antecedents', *Harvard Studies in Classical Philology* 82 (1978), pp. 213-63. One of the most important essays on the traditions of ancient drama which shaped Senecan theatre.

N.T. Pratt, *Seneca's Drama* (Chapel Hill & London: University of North Carolina Press, 1983). Offers a helpful general account of the plays, with an emphasis upon their philosophical subtext.

D. and E. Henry, *The Mask of Power: Seneca's Tragedies and Imperial Rome* (Warminster: Aris & Phillips, 1985).

A.J. Boyle, *Tragic Seneca: an Essay in the Theatrical Tradition* (London: Routledge, 1997). Provides a general account of Seneca's influence on Renaissance drama.

On the decline of formal drama, and on recitation

See the article on *recitatio* in the *OCD* for the practice of recitation generally.

L. Friedländer, *Roman Life and Manners under the Early Empire* (London: Routledge & Kegan Paul, 1913). Much useful material on literary matters in volumes ii.95-9 and iv.255-6, and on dramas composed for reading see ii.447 and 621.

R.C. Beacham, *The Roman Theatre and its Audience* (London & New York: Routledge, 1991), pp. 125-6 briefly chart the decline of tragedies composed for the stage, and conclude that Seneca wrote for recitation and publication.

E. Csapo and W.J. Slater, *The Context of Ancient Drama* (Ann Arbor: University of Michigan Press, 1995). A very useful source book, which however does not note that some ancient dramas were composed with a view to recitation.

Sander M. Goldberg, 'The Fall and Rise of Roman Tragedy', *Transactions of the American Philological Association* 126 (1996), pp. 265-86. A very important essay.

D.F. Sutton, *Seneca on the Stage* (*Mnemosyne* Supplement 96, Leiden: E.J. Brill, 1986). Argues the case for performance; he devotes a section of his study to the implicit stage directions to be deduced from the text. This is an unexceptionable strategy, but only partial. The chief problems of staging arise rather from the lack of even implicit directions where they are needed (for example, the question of when the corpse of Hippolytus appears on stage). He deals with *Phaedra* on pp. 50-3.

Guide to Further Reading

On the Chorus

Peter J. Davis, *Shifting Song: the Chorus in Seneca's Tragedies* (Altertumswissenschaftliche Texte und Studien 26; Hildesheim: Olms-Weidmann, 1993). Discusses the Chorus in our play throughout his study (which unhelpfully has no index). He argues for its presence or absence on stage on pp. 21-2 and 28-31 (largely an expanded repetition of the previous discussion). For its character, which he reads as hostile to Phaedra, see pp. 52-4. He discusses the use of mythology in the first and second choral odes on pp. 93-104, and the philosophical content of the third and fourth odes on pp. 146-56. The dramatic use of the Chorus is described on pp. 227-30, and an appreciation of the poetry of the third ode is to be found on pp. 252-4.

On characterisation

S.G. Flyght, 'Treatment of character in Euripides and Seneca: *The Hippolytus*', *Classical Journal* 29 (1933-34), pp. 507-16. Old-fashioned, but tidy comparison of the characters.

Michael Coffey, Introduction to Coffey and Mayer (editors), *Seneca: Phaedra*, pp. 26-8. A brisk account.

F. Ahl's translation of our play (see above) has a brief section on the characters, pp. 38-41, in which some alert points are suggested for discussion. Ahl does however fall into the old-fashioned error of treating dramatic characters as real people. We know no more about Hippolytus than the words on the page tell us. It is pointless to ask, as Ahl does, if there is a possibility of his feeling and repressing a desire for Phaedra, since there is nothing in the text to suggest such a reading of his character. Similarly, we simply cannot know if Phaedra has a 'genuine' concern for the Nurse when she offers to reveal her secret to Theseus. It is not something Seneca has given us any clues about.

F. Tealdo, 'Personaggi e funzioni nella *Phaedra* di Seneca', *Aufidus* 16 (1992), pp. 77-121. A structuralist reading of characterisation: Do the character traits of the individuals establish their functions, or does their function prompt the introduction and creation of their parts?

F. Dupont, 'Le prologue de la *Phèdre* de Sénèque', *Revue des Études Latines* 69 (1991), pp. 124-35. The character of Hippolytus, as revealed in the prologue.

O. Zwierlein, *Senecas Phaedra und ihre Vorbilder* (Akademie der Wissenschaften und der Literatur – Mainz: Abhandlungen der

Geistes- und Sozialwissenschaftlichen Klasse 5; Stuttgart: Franz
Steiner, 1987). The character of Phaedra as a wanton manipulator.

On literary indebtedness

R.J. Tarrant, 'Greek and Roman in Seneca's Tragedies', *Harvard Studies in Classical Philology* 97 (1995), pp. 215-30. Fundamental, and note especially p. 223: 'At the level of detailed verbal interaction, the texts which Seneca most closely engages in dialogue are more often Roman than Greek.'

M.C.J. Putnam, 'Virgil's tragic future: Senecan drama and the *Aeneid*', in *Virgil's Aeneid: Interpretation and Influence* (Chapel Hill & London: University of North Carolina Press, 1995), pp. 265-6. On Seneca's 'reading' of Virgil's *Aeneid*; he is mainly concerned with how the very final scene of the *Aeneid*, with its emphasis on *ira*, *furor*, *dolor*, impressed itself upon Seneca's imagination to the extent that these themes dominate his tragic output.

R. Jakobi, *Der Einfluss Ovids auf den Tragiker Seneca* (Untersuchungen zur antiken Literatur und Geschichte 28; Berlin & New York: De Gruyter, 1988). The pervasive influence of Ovid upon *Phaedra* is discussed – atomically rather than synthetically – on pp. 63-89. See too the seven-page appendix of examples drawn from numerous poets in Coffey and Mayer, *Seneca: Phaedra*.

On visual representation of the myth

Jane Davidson Reid (editor), *Oxford Guide to Classical Myth in the Arts* (Oxford: Oxford University Press, 1993). Indispensable: see vol. ii.883-8 s.v. 'Phaedra and Hippolytus'. Most of the later indebtedness is to either Euripides or Racine, but some is to Seneca; a fair number of items betray no indication of which texts were most influential. (Jean-Jacques Lagrenée the Younger's painting of 1795 in the St Petersburg Hermitage, formerly entitled 'Phaedra accusing Hippolytus before Theseus', has been renamed in the 1987 catalogue of the collection.)

On performance

All who want information on the performance history of classical drama should consult the Oxford University Archive of Performances of Greek and Roman Drama, 67 St Giles, Oxford OX1 3LU; apgrd@lithum.ox.ac.uk; http://www.classics.ox.ac.uk/apgrd/. Over thirty performances of *Phaedra* between 1474 to 2000 are known.

D. Ardini 'Proposta di messa in scena della Fedra', in *Atti dei convegni 'Il mondo scenico di Plauto' e 'Seneca e i volti del potere'* (Pubblicazioni del Dipartimento di Archeologia, Filologia Classica e loro Tradizioni, n.s. 160; Genoa: Brigati Glauco, 1995), pp. 207-18. Argues for the greater openness of the modern day to Senecan dramaturgy; on pp. 212-18 she sets out her own scheme for performance.

M.D. Grant, 'Plautus and Seneca: Acting in Nero's Rome', *Greece and Rome* 46 (1999), pp. 27-33. Offers some reflections on the continuity of performance practice in Rome.

Addendum

The first volume of the Loeb Classical Library edition of Seneca's tragedies has just been replaced by a newly edited text and translation by J.G. Fitch; there is a 33-page general introduction and bibliography, and each play is given its own brief introduction and special bibliography.

Sarah Kane's play, *Phaedra's Love*, was reprinted in 2000 with minor revisions she made before her death; that edition is therefore definitive.

Bibliography

F. Ahl, *Seneca. Three Tragedies* (Ithaca & London: Cornell University Press, 1986).
U. Albini, *Viaggio nel teatro classico* (Florence: Le Monnier, 1987), pp. 146-54.
F. Amoroso, 'Messa in scena di Seneca tragico', *Dioniso* 63.2 (1993), pp. 87-100.
A. Andrisano, *Fedra, Dioniso* 65.1-2 (1995), pp. 90-3.
D. Ardini, 'Proposta di messa in scena della Fedra', in *Atti dei convegni 'Il mondo scenico di Plauto' e 'Seneca e i volti del potere'* (Pubblicazioni del Dipartimento di Archeologia, Filologia Classica e loro Tradizioni, n.s. 160; Genoa: Brigati Glauco, 1995), pp. 207-18.
M. Armisen-Marchetti, 'Pour une lecture des tragédies de Sénèque. L'exemple de *Phèdre*, v. 130-135', *Pallas* 38 (1992), pp. 379-90.
E.V. Arnold, *Roman Stoicism* (Cambridge: Cambridge University Press, 1911).
C. Barone, 'Un recente allestimento della *Fedra* di Seneca', *Dioniso* 52 (1981), pp. 449-53.
W.S. Barrett (editor), *Euripides Hippolytos* (Oxford: Clarendon Press, 1964).
V.C. Barsan, *Garnier and Seneca* (Dissertation, University of Illinois, 1965, published by University Microfilms in 1965).
R.C. Beacham, *The Roman Theatre and its Audience* (London & New York: Routledge, 1991).
────── *Spectacle Entertainments of Early Imperial Rome* (New Haven & London: Yale University Press, 1999).
W. Beare, *The Roman Stage*[3] (London: Methuen & Co. Ltd., 1964).
P.G. Bietenholz and T.B. Deutscher (editors), *Contemporaries of Erasmus: a Biographical Register of the Renaissance and Reformation* (Toronto, Buffalo & London: University of Toronto Press, 1986).
J.W. Binns, 'William Gager's Additions to Seneca's *Hippolytus*', *Studies in the Renaissance* 17 (1970), pp. 153-91.
F.S. Boas, *University Drama in the Tudor Age* (Oxford: Clarendon Press, 1914).

Seneca: Phaedra

A. Borgo, *Lessico parentale in Seneca tragico* (Naples: Loffredo, 1993).
M. Bowie, *Lacan* (Cambridge, MA & London: Harvard University Press, 1991).
A.J. Boyle (editor), *Seneca Tragicus* (RAMUS Essays on Senecan Drama; Berwick: Aureal Publications, 1983).
────── 'In Nature's Bonds: a Study of Seneca's *Phaedra*', in H. Temporini (editor), *Aufstieg und Niedergang der römischen Welt* II 32.2 (Berlin & New York: De Gruyter, 1985), pp. 1284-347.
────── *Seneca's Phaedra* (Latin and Greek Texts, 5; Liverpool: Francis Cairns, 1987).
────── *Tragic Seneca: an Essay in the Theatrical Tradition* (London: Routledge, 1997).
F. Caviglia, 'La morte di Ippolito nella *Fedra* di Seneca', *Quaderni di Cultura e di Tradizione Classica* 8 (1990), pp. 119-33.
────── 'Commenti di ecclesiastici a Seneca Tragico: Trevet e Delrio', *Aevum Antiquum* 13 (2000), pp. 351-63.
P. Claes, *Claus-reading* (Amsterdam, 1984).
────── *De mot zit in de mythe* (Amsterdam, 1984).
H. Claus, *Phaedra (naar Seneca)* (Amsterdam: International Theatre and Film Books, 1995).
M. Coffey and R. Mayer (editors), *Seneca: Phaedra* (Cambridge Greek and Latin Classics: Cambridge: Cambridge University Press, 1990).
J.M. Cooper and J.F. Procopé, *Seneca, Moral and Political Essays* (Cambridge: Cambridge University Press, 1995).
C.D.N. Costa (editor), *Seneca* (London & Boston: Routledge & Kegan Paul, 1974).
W.M.A. Creizenach, *Geschichte des neueren Dramas* (Halle: Max Niemeyer, 1918, 2nd edition).
M.G. Critelli, 'L'Arcadia impossibile: elementi di un'età dell'oro nella *Phaedra* di Seneca', *Rivista di cultura classica e medioevale* 40 (1998), pp. 71-6.
────── 'Ideologia e simbologia della natura nella *Phaedra* di Seneca', *Rivista di cultura classica e medioevale* 41 (1999), pp. 233-43.
F. Cruciani, *Teatro nel Rinascimento: Roma 1450-1550* (Rome: Bulzoni, 1983).
E. Csapo and W.J. Slater, *The Context of Ancient Drama* (Ann Arbor: University of Michigan Press, 1995).
D. Dalla Valle, *Gli 'Hippolytes' senechiani del teatro francese* (Turin, 1986).
────── *Quando Ippolito s'innamora* (Turin, 1990).
S. D'Amico (editor), *Enciclopedia dello Spettacolo* (Rome: Le Maschere, 1954-66).
M. David, 'Mito e tragedie di Fedra nella letteratura psicanalitica', *Quaderni dannunziani* 5-6 (1989), 22-3.

Bibliography

P.J. Davis, 'Vindicat Omnes Natura Sibi: a Reading of Seneca's *Phaedra*' in Boyle, *Seneca Tragicus*, pp. 114-27.

——— *Shifting Song: the Chorus in Seneca's Tragedies* (Altertumswissenschaftliche Texte und Studien 26; Hildesheim: Olms-Weidmann, 1993).

——— 'Rewriting Seneca: Garnier's *Hippolyte*', *Classical and Modern Literature* 17.4 (1997), pp. 293-318.

P.-A. Deproost, 'Le martyre chez Prudence: sagesse et tragédie. La reception de Sénèque dans le Peristephanon Liber', *Philologus* 143 (1999), pp. 161-80.

M. Dietrich, 'Pomponius Laetus Wiederentdeckung des antiken Theaters', *Maske und Kothurn* 3 (1957), pp. 245-67.

W. Doyle, *Jansenism: Catholic Resistance to Authority from the Reformation to the French Revolution* (Studies in European History; Basingstoke: Macmillan, 2000).

F. Dupont, 'Le prologue de la Phèdre de Sénèque', *Revue des Études Latines* 69 (1991), pp. 124-35.

T.S. Eliot, 'Seneca in Elizabethan Translation', in *Selected Essays* (London: Faber & Faber, 1961), pp. 65-105.

W. Evenpoel, 'Le martyre dans le Peristephanon Liber de Prudence', *Sacris Eruditi* 36 (1996), pp. 5-35.

V. Faggi, 'Il personaggio di Fedra nella tragedia di Seneca', in *Atti dei convegni 'Il mondo scenico di Plauto' e 'Seneca e i volti del potere'* (Pubblicazioni del Dipartimento di Archeologia, Filologia Classica e loro Tradizioni, n.s. 160; Genoa: Brigati Glauco, 1995), pp. 201-6.

E. Fantham, 'Virgil's Dido and Seneca's Tragic Heroines', *Greece and Rome* 22 (1975), pp. 1-10.

——— 'Production of Seneca's *Trojan Women*, Ancient? and Modern' in Harrison, *Seneca in Performance*, pp. 13-26.

J.G. Fitch, 'Sense Pauses and Relative Dating in Seneca, Sophocles and Shakespeare', *American Journal of Philology* 102 (1981), pp. 289-307.

——— 'Playing Seneca?' in Harrison, *Seneca in Performance*, pp. 1-12.

S.G. Flygt, 'Treatment of Character in Euripides and Seneca: The *Hippolytus*', *Classical Journal* 29 (1933-34), pp. 507-16.

S. Fortey and J. Glucker, 'Actus Tragicus: Seneca on the Stage', *Latomus* 34 (1975), pp. 699-715.

D. Fowler, 'Reading Senecan Tragedy', in *Unrolling the Text: Books and Readers in Roman Poetry* (Oxford: Oxford University Press, 2002).

L. Friedländer, *Roman Life and Manners under the Early Empire* (London: Routledge & Kegan Paul, 1913).

J.J. Gahan, '*Imitatio* and *Aemulatio* in Seneca's *Phaedra*', *Latomus* 46 (1987), pp. 380-7.

G. Garbarino, 'La *Fedra* di Seneca e alcune tragedie francesi del

Seicento', *Quaderni di Cultura e di Tradizione Classica* 19 (1992), pp. 277-89.

F. Gasti, 'La "passione" di Ippolito: Seneca e Prudenzio', *Quaderni di Cultura e di Tradizione Classica* 11 (1993), pp. 215-28.

R. Gazich, 'La *Fedra* di Seneca tra *pathos* ed elegia', *Humanitas (Brescia)* 52 (1997), pp. 348-75.

P. Ghiron-Bistagne, 'Il motivo di Fedra nell'iconografia e la *Fedra* di Seneca', *Dioniso* 52 (1985), pp. 261-306.

F. Giancotti, *Poesia e filosofia in Seneca tragico, la Fedra* (Turin: CELID, 1986).

——— 'Profilo della *Fedra* di Seneca con raffronti dannunziani specie in rapporto al finale', in *Fedra da Euripide a D'Annunzio, Quaderni dannunziani* 5-6 (1989), pp. 51-75.

S.M. Goldberg, 'The Fall and Rise of Roman Tragedy', *Transactions of the American Philological Association* 126 (1996), pp. 265-86.

M.D. Grant, 'Plautus and Seneca: Acting in Nero's Rome', *Greece and Rome* 46 (1999), pp. 27-33.

M.T. Griffin, *Seneca, a Philosopher in Politics* (Oxford: Clarendon Press, 1976).

P. Grimal, 'L'originalité de Sénèque dans la tragédie de Phèdre', *Revue des Études Latines* 41 (1963), pp. 297-314 (= *Rome: la littérature et l'histoire* [Rome: École française de Rome, 1986], i.557-73).

G.W.M. Harrison (editor), *Seneca in Performance* (London: Duckworth / Classical Press of Wales, 2000).

D. Henry and B. Walker, 'Phantasmagoria and Idyll: an Element of Seneca's *Phaedra*', *Greece and Rome* 13 (1966), pp. 223-9.

D. and E. Henry, *The Mask of Power: Seneca's Tragedies and Imperial Rome* (Warminster: Aris & Phillips, 1985).

P. Heuzé, 'Les aveux de Phèdre' in R. Chevalier and R. Poignault (editors), *Présence de Sénèque* (Paris: Touzot, 1991), pp. 171-8.

H.M. Hine (editor), *Seneca Medea* (Warminster: Aris & Phillips, 2000).

A. Hollingsworth, 'Recitation Poetry and Seneca's Tragedies. Is There a Similarity?', *Classical World* 94 (2001), pp. 135-44.

G.O. Hutchinson, *Latin Literature from Seneca to Juvenal* (Oxford: Clarendon Press, 1993), pp. 160-4.

J. Jacquot (editor), *Les tragédies de Sénèque et le théâtre de la Renaissance* (Paris: Centre National pour la Recherche Scientifique, 1964).

R. Jakobi, *Der Einfluss Ovids auf den Tragiker Seneca* (Untersuchungen zur antiken Literatur und Geschichte 28; Berlin & New York: De Gruyter, 1988).

E. James and G. Jondorf, *Racine Phèdre* (Landmarks of World Literature, Cambridge: Cambridge University Press, 1994).

S. Kane, *Phaedra's Love* (London: Methuen, 1996).

Bibliography

H.A. Kelly, 'Tragedy and the Performance of Tragedy in Late Roman Antiquity', *Traditio* 35 (1979), pp. 21-44.

P. Kragelund, 'Senecan Tragedy: Back on Stage?', *Classica et Mediaevalia* 50 (1999), pp. 239-43.

J. Lapp, *Aspects of Racinian Tragedy* (University of Toronto Romance Series; Toronto: University of Toronto Press, 1955, reprinted 1964).

V.T. Larson, *The Role of Description in Senecan Tragedy* (Frankfurt, etc.: Peter Lang, 1994).

C. Lazzarini, *Ovidio: Rimedi contro L'Amore* (Venice: Marsilio, 1986).

A.D. Leeman, 'Seneca's *Phaedra* as a Stoic Tragedy', in J.M. Bremer, S.L. Radt and C.J. Ruijgh (editors), *Miscellanea Tragica in Honorem J.C. Kamerbeek* (Amsterdam: A. Hakkert, 1976), pp. 199-212.

E. Lefèvre, *'Quid ratio possit?* Senecas *Phaedra* als stoisches Drama', *Wiener Studien* 3 (1969), pp. 131-60.

—— (editor), *Senecas Tragödien* (Wege der Forschung 310; Darmstadt: Wissenschaftliche Buchgesellschaft, 1972).

—— (editor), *Der Einfluss Senecas auf das europäische Drama* (Darmstadt: Wissenschaftliche Buchgesellschaft, 1978).

—— 'Die Monomanie der senecanischen Phaedra', *Quaderni di Cultura e di Tradizione Classica* 4-5 (1987), pp. 207-17.

—— 'Die politische Bedeutung von Senecas *Phaedra*', *Wiener Studien* 24 (1990), pp. 109-22.

F. Leo, *L. Annaei Senecae Tragoediae* (Berlin: Weidmann, 1879).

S. Lerer, *Boethius and Dialogue: Literary Method in the Consolation of Philosophy* (Princeton: Princeton University Press, 1985).

L.A. Mackay, 'The Roman Tragic Spirit', in *California Studies in Classical Antiquity* 8 (1975), pp. 145-62.

S. Marchitelli, 'Nicholas Trevet und die Renaissance der Senecas Tragödien', *Museum Helveticum* 56 (1999), pp. 36-63, 87-104.

G. Mastromarco, *The Public of Herondas* (Amsterdam: J.C. Gieben, 1984).

C. Maxia, 'Seneca e l'età d'oro', *Bolletino di Studi Latini* 30 (2000), pp. 87-105.

R.G. Mayer, 'Neronian Classicism', *American Journal of Philology* 103 (1983), pp. 305-18.

—— 'Doctus Seneca', *Mnemosyne* 43 (1990), pp. 395-407.

—— 'Personata Stoa: Neostoicism and Senecan Tragedy', *Journal of the Warburg and Courtauld Institutes* 57 (1994), pp. 154-5.

R.F. Merzlak, '*Furor* in Seneca's *Phaedra*', in C. Deroux (editor), *Studies in Latin Literature and Roman History* (Collection Latomus 180; Brussels: Latomus, 1983), iii.193-210.

F.J. Miller, *Seneca Tragedies* (Chicago: University of Chicago Press, 1907), reprinted in G.E. Duckworth (editor), *The Complete Roman Drama* (New York: Random House, 1942), vol. 2.

Seneca: Phaedra

——— *Seneca Tragedies* (Loeb Classical Library; Cambridge, MA: Harvard University Press, 1917).
U. Moricca, 'Le fonti della *Fedra* di Seneca', *Studi italiani di filologia classica* 21 (1915), pp. 158-224.
M. Mueller, *Children of Oedipus and Other Essays on the Imitation of Greek Tragedy, 1550-1800* (Toronto: University of Toronto Press, 1980).
R.A.B. Mynors (editor), *Collected Works of Erasmus: Correspondence.* vol. 9 (Toronto, Buffalo & London: University of Toronto Press, 1989).
W. Newton, *Le thème de Phèdre et d'Hippolyte dans la littérature française* (Paris: E. Droz, 1939).
H.L. Nostrand, *Le Théâtre antique et à l'antique en France de 1840 à 1900* (Paris: E. Droz, 1934).
G.J.P. O'Daly, *The Poetry of Boethius* (London: Duckworth, 1991).
F. Orlando, *Toward a Freudian Theory of Literature* (Baltimore & London: Johns Hopkins University Press, 1978).
J.M. Osho, 'Variations on the Phaedra Theme in Euripides, Seneca and Racine', *Nigeria and the Classics* 12 (1970), pp. 86-101.
R. van der Paardt, *Antieke motieven in de moderne Nederlandse letterkunde, een eigentijdse Odyssee* (Amsterdam, 1982).
——— *Mythe en metamorfose, klassieke themas en motieven in de moderne literatuur* (Amsterdam, 1991).
A.-M. Palmer, *Prudentius on the Martyrs* (Oxford: Clarendon Press, 1989).
E. Paratore, 'La morte di Fedra in Seneca e nel D'Annunzio' in V. Gabrieli (editor), *Friendship's Garland: Essays ... Mario Praz* (Rome: Edizioni di Storia e Letteratura, 1966), pp. 413-34.
M. Paschalis, 'The Bull and the Horse: Animal Theme and Imagery in Seneca's *Phaedra*', *American Journal of Philology* 115 (1994), pp. 105-28.
F. Pintor, *Rappresentazioni romane di Seneca e Plauto nel Rinascimento* (Perugia, 1906).
J. Pommier, *Aspects de Racine* (Paris: Librairie Nizet, 1954).
N.T. Pratt, *Seneca's Drama* (Chapel Hill & London: University of North Carolina Press, 1983).
M.C.J. Putnam, *Virgil's Aeneid: Interpretation and Influence* (Chapel Hill & London: University of North Carolina Press, 1995).
O. Rank, *The Incest Theme in Literature and Legend* (Baltimore: Johns Hopkins University Press, 1992).
B.R. Rees, 'English Seneca: a Preamble', *Greece and Rome* 16 (1969), p. 123.
O. Regenbogen, 'Schmerz und Tod in den Tragödien Senecas', *Vorträge der Bibliothek Warburg 1927-1928* (1930), pp. 167-218.

Bibliography

J.D. Reid (editor), *Oxford Guide to Classical Myth in the Arts* (Oxford: Oxford University Press, 1993).

M.R. Rivoltella, 'Il motivo della colpa ereditaria nelle tragedie senecane: una ciclicità in "crescendo" ', *Aevum* 67 (1993), pp. 113-28.

M.J. Roberts, *Poetry and the Cult of the Martyrs: the Liber Peristephanon of Prudentius* (Ann Arbor: University of Michigan Press, 1993).

H.M. Roisman, *Nothing is as it Seems: the Tragedy of the Implicit in Euripides' Hippolytus* (Lanham, MD & Oxford: Rowman & Littlefield, 1999).

——— 'A New Look at Seneca's *Phaedra*' in Harrison, *Seneca in Performance*, pp. 73-86.

F.H. Sandbach, *The Stoics* (Ancient Culture and Society; London: Chatto & Windus, 1975).

P. Schlicke (editor), *Oxford Reader's Companion to Dickens* (Oxford: Oxford University Press, 1999).

J.U. Schmidt, 'Phaedra und der Einfluss ihrer Amme: zum Sieg des mythischen Weltbildes über die Philosophie in Senecas *Phaedra*', *Philologus* 139 (1995), pp. 274-323.

C.P. Segal, 'Dissonant Sympathy: Song, Orpheus and the Golden Age in Seneca's Tragedies', in Boyle, *Seneca Tragicus*, pp. 244-9.

——— *Language and Desire in Seneca's Phaedra* (Princeton: Princeton University Press, 1984).

D. Share (editor), *Seneca in English* (Harmondsworth: Penguin, 1998).

R.W. Sharples, *Stoics, Epicureans and Sceptics: an Introduction to Hellenistic Philosophy* (London & New York: Routledge, 1996).

A. Sierz, *In Yer Face Theatre: British Drama Today* (London: Faber & Faber, 2001).

D.R. Slavitt and Palmer Bovie (editors), *Seneca, The Tragedies*, vol. 1 (Complete Roman Drama in Translation; Baltimore & London: Johns Hopkins University Press, 1992).

B.R. Smith, *Ancient Scripts and Modern Experience on the English Stage 1500-1700* (Princeton: Princeton University Press, 1988).

W.C. Summers (editor), *Select Letters of Seneca* (London: Macmillan, 1910).

D.F. Sutton, *Seneca on the Stage* (*Mnemosyne* Supplement 96; Leiden: E.J. Brill, 1986).

R.J. Tarrant, 'Senecan Drama and its Antecedents', *Harvard Studies in Classical Philology* 82 (1978), pp. 213-63.

——— 'The Younger Seneca: Tragedies', in L.D. Reynolds (editor), *Texts and Transmission: a Survey of the Latin Classics* (Oxford: Clarendon Press, 1986 corrected edition), pp. 378-81.

——— 'Greek and Roman in Seneca's Tragedies', *Harvard Studies in Classical Philology* 97 (1995), pp. 215-30.

F. Tealdo, 'Personaggi e funzioni nella *Phaedra* di Seneca', *Aufidus* 16 (1992), pp. 77-121.

R.W. Tobin, *Racine and Seneca* (University of North Carolina Studies in the Romance Languages and Literatures 96; Chapel Hill: University of North Carolina Press, 1971).

W. Trillitzsch, 'Seneca tragicus – Nachleben und Beurteilung im lateinischen Mittelalter von der Spätantike bis zum Renaissancehumanismus', in *Philologus* 122 (1978), pp. 134-5.

R. Trombino, 'Phaedra on the stage: sul recente allestimento della *Phaedra* di Seneca a cura di Franco Ricordi', *Dioniso* 58 (1988), pp. 137-40.

H.J. Tschiedel, 'La *Fedra* di Seneca: una lettura', *Aevum Antiquum* 10 (1997), pp. 337-53.

E.F. Watling, *Seneca: Four Tragedies and Octavia* (Harmondsworth: Penguin, 1966).

P.J. Willetts, *Catalogue of the Manuscripts in the Society of Antiquaries of London* (London: D.S. Brewer for the Society, 2000).

B. Williams, *Shame and Necessity* (Berkeley & London: University of California Press, 1993).

G. Williams, 'Poet and Audience in Senecan Tragedy: *Phaedra* 358-430', in T. Woodman and J. Powell (editors), *Author and Audience in Latin Literature* (Cambridge: Cambridge University Press, 1992), pp. 138-49.

F. Zoccali, 'Il prologo "allegorico" della *Phaedra* di Seneca', in *Bolletino di Studi Latini* 27 (1997), pp. 433-53.

O. Zwierlein, *L. Annaei Senecae Tragoediae* (Oxford Classical Text; Oxford, 1986).

―――― *Senecas Phaedra und ihre Vorbilder* (Akademie der Wissenschaften und der Literatur – Mainz: Abhandlungen der Geistes- und Sozialwissenschaftlichen Klasse 5; Stuttgart: Franz Steiner, 1987).

Chronology

4 BC – AD 1: Period within which Seneca was born.
49-54: Period within which *Phaedra* is likely to have been composed and first performed at a recitation.
65: Suicide of Seneca.
1486?: First performance of *Phaedra* in Latin in the modern day, at Rome. Subsequently performances are recorded for other parts of Italy, and for Northern Europe.
1546 (Christmas): Performance of *Phaedra* in Latin, as *Hippolytus*, at Westminster School, near London.
1554: Performance of *Phaedra* in Latin at Wittenberg in Germany.
1583 (Shrove Tuesday, 8 February): Performance at Christ Church, Oxford.
1969: Staging of Sanguineti's translation produced by Luca Ronconi in Rome.
1973: Performance in Latin by the Classical Society of Exeter University, UK.
1980: Claus' Dutch adaptation written.
1981: Staging of Faggi's Italian translation.
1995 (25 March): Staging of Claus' adaptation by Het Zuidelijk Toneel, Eindhoven, Holland. The production was taken on tour.
1995 (7 July): Staging of scenes at Bologna.

Index

Accius, 14-15
Aeschylus, 66
allusiveness, 73-4
Aristotle, 16, 91
asides, 24-5

Bidar, 79
blending of sources, 65-8
Boethius, 77

Celtis, C., 100
Chorus, 22, 23, 32-5, 41, 127
Cicero, Q., 14
Claus, H., 25, 79, 84-5
contaminatio, 65
Corneille, P., 81

D'Annunzio, G., 84
death on stage, 31
Dickens, C., 97-8

Eber, P., 100
Ennius, 13
ellipse, 72-3
epigram, 74
Erasmus, D., 99
Euripides, 13, 23, 25-6, 28, 32, 45-7, 51, 54, 56, 58, 59, 61, 62, 66, 67, 68, 69, 78, 80, 81, 83, 84, 86, 114, 115

fortune, 11, 29, 33, 45, 77

Gager, W., 101
Garnier, R., 25, 78-9, 82, 85
gods, 45-7
Golden Age, 23, 39, 54-5, 57, 70
Gravelot, H., 83

heredity, 40-1, 60, 79
Horace 31-2 (*Ars Poetica*), 54, 66, 70
humour, 70
hunting, 54-5
hyperbaton, 110

imitation (literary), 23, 32, 65, 128
incest, 19, 38, 39-40, 72, 79, 87, 93
Inghirami, T., 100

Jansenism, 80

Kane, S., 84, 85-7

La Pinelière, 79
Leto, P., 99
Lucan, 45, 48, 109

madness, 19, 42-4
mime, 15
misogyny, 47, 55, 61, 63, 72, 93

nature, 11, 23, 37-9, 72

Index

Nero, 10, 11, 13
Nowell, A., 90

Ovid, 15 (*Medea*), 26 (*Heroides 4*), 28, 43, 54, 67, 70-1, 72, 109, 112 (*Remedia Amoris*), 128

pantomime, 15, 120
passion, 11
Petronius, 44
phantasia, 16
Piccolomini, A.S., 78
Plato, 66
Plautus, 65
Pollio, 14, 97
Pomponius Secundus, 76
providence, 11
Prudentius, 76
psychoanalysis, 92-5

Quintilian, 11, 12-13, 76, 122

Racine, J., 27, 53, 61, 62, 79-83
realism, 46, 52, 53, 55, 58, 60
reason, 11, 39, 42-4, 53
recitation, 14, 16-17, 25, 97-8
rhetoric, 62-3, 71-2, 93, 94

Riario, R., 99-100, 121

Servius, 89
Sotion, 54
Sophocles, 31, 60, 66, 67, 69
staging difficulties, 24-5, 30-1, 52-3, 58, 79, 107-9, 126
Stoicism, 10, 37-8, 41, 42, 44, 45, 48, 53, 72, 90-2, 115
Studley, J., 105
style, 72-3
suasoria, 71
Sulpizio, G.A., 99-100
Swinburne, A.C., 83-4

Tacitus, 48
Terence, 65
Thomas, D., 17
Trevet, N., 78, 89-90

Varius' *Thyestes*, 15
Virgil, 65, 69, 70, 109, 128
virginity, 20, 47, 55, 57
virtue, 11, 29
Vondel, J. van den, 85

woods, 19, 21, 22, 23, 24, 29, 38-9, 43, 47, 56, 85, 103